——THE——
UNQUIET
SUITCASE

GERALD PRIESTLAND

THE UNQUIET SUITCASE

Priestland at Sixty

ANDRE DEUTSCH

First published October 1988 by
André Deutsch Limited
105 - 106 Great Russell Street
London WC1B 3LJ
Second impression October 1988

British Library Cataloguing in Publication Data

Priestland, Gerald, 1927–
    The unquiet suitcase: Priestland at 60.
    1. Great Britain. Radio & television
    Programmes. Broadcasting. Priestland,
    Gerald, 1927, Biographies
    I. Title
    791.44′092′4

ISBN 0–233–98329–5

Phototypeset by Falcon Graphic Art Ltd
Wallington, Surrey
Printed in Great Britain by
Billing & Sons Limited, Worcester

To the Two Jennets

February 25th 1987

Seven of us sit in a BBC basement looking like a parochial church council. Libby Purves is in the chair as vicar's wife; Tom Davies, a Welsh writer I've reviewed with approval; Midweek's resident poetaster; a couple called Cooper, in the process of sailing rather slowly round the world (an activity almost certain to get you on the air); Rosemary Hartill, my successor as religious correspondent; and a duckologist – a man with thirty-two ducks in his garden. He says his two daughters are fed up with the birds and say unbroadcastable things about them. Go on, whispers my demon, you say 'Fuck the ducks?' But I don't.

I don't think it was very objective of the producer to get Rosemary to do my sixtieth birthday interview. When Q. and A. know each other too well, it tends to make the listener feel left out. Colleagues ought not to interview one another if 'the truth' is to be extracted without favour. But do I want 'the truth' to come out? Rose treats me very gently, as if it were downhill all the way to the cemetery, which is rather how I feel. I have slept badly and do not sparkle. A lot of tired old anecdotes tumble out touching their forelocks. Still, if I decline to do a striptease, at least I give Midweek a dance.

In the waiting room Chris Rees and Caroline Millington – old collaborators – look in to wish me well. I kiss Caro and Rose and Libby but not Christopher. The Coopers are impressed. I tell them I picked up this enjoyable custom from cousins who were famed in Berkhamsted as 'the kissing Coopers'. They'd kiss anyone in reach.

Midweek play an old tape of me sounding a fanfare on four trombones. It was arranged by Caroline's mate Mike Robinson to sabotage the network on a dull night. Radio 4 continuity used to steal half a minute of our programme to play silly jingles, so on that occasion we got in first with one of our own and left them speechless.

After Midweek I walk across Regent's Park to St John's Wood parish church for the funeral of a suicide: Martin (let's call him) who shot himself at the age of thirty after a hellish life of schizophrenia. We sing three or four good hymns and listen to a couple of eulogists doing their best to avoid saying the worst. I think it was all bound to end as it did. Martin's family deserve much credit for keeping him alive as long as they did. Schizophrenia is a frightful scourge for which (unlike depression) there seems little hope.

Then I go home and hack out a thousand well-paid words for one of the newspapers about women priests. Poor old radio cannot compete with Fleet Street's fees, I'm afraid. But I still love the medium of sound. It brings out the subtle rhythms of the English language and, frankly, it does help to advertise one's wares.

Tomorrow really *is* my birthday.

February 26th

Kobbe's *Complete Opera Book* weighs four pounds and feels more when laid on the chest in the early morning. 'Happy birthday,' from Sylvia, 'but don't expect another present like that for another ten years.' I browse happily through the preposterous plots, before remembering it is women priests' day at the General Synod. How better to pass one's birthday? So off to Church House, next to Westminster

Abbey, and up into the gallery to find the ecclesiastical press corps has not altered much since I retired from it officially. But the whiff of sex and schism has drawn in reinforcements of bewildered young people from the popular press who have to be told what a prebendary is and warned that whatever happens there won't be a woman vicar for another five years at least.

Graham Leonard, Bishop of London and leader of the resistance against the Monstrous Regiment, is in surprisingly low form after all his threats of pushing off to find better company among the Romans or the Orthodox. He looks depressed, stares into his lap and speaks inaudibly and without fire. A strange man who, I suspect, has never forgiven himself for discovering the Catholic way rather late in the day. Undoubtedly sincere, but with a glint of fanaticism. Once, when he was Bishop of Truro, he told me that the problem really bothering his Cornish flock was 'oral sex'. People kept asking him should they do it?

The abbot-like Father Brian Brindley ('the Great Amender' as I once christened him) does his best to wreck the bishops' scheme for bringing in women – but time after time, Synod slaps him down. Bob Runcie (the Archb. of C.) is in excellent, incisive form, doing his best to calm the war of nerves the anti-womenites have stirred up. 'It's a little early', he observes, 'to be taking the tarpaulins off the lifeboats or even to start signalling to other shipping to stand by to take off some of the passengers.' Leonard, at whom this is aimed, fails to join the laughter. But Brindley – who has been taking huge pleasure in enunciating words like 'episcopate' and 'episcopacy' without falling over – says he isn't looking for lifeboats, he's battening down the hatches.

About the only new feature of the debate is wee John Gummer playing the parliamentary card. Synod is not all that heartbroken by his announcement that a Church of England with women priests will be a Church of England without John Gummer; but there is a slight chill when he warns that if it tries to sneak the principle through without stating the details, parliament will smell a rat and cry 'Foul!' Synod likes to think of itself as sovereign and doesn't care to be reminded there is still a political veto across the road. Fortunately an able lawyer called Bullimore speaks next and says he hopes members 'won't fall for Mr Gummer'. There is no reason why parliament should not be shown the whole package. Gummer is comforted by a lady with a defiant hat and a fierce Tory voice.

In the end the bishops' plan (a sort of White Paper, really) is passed handsomely by all three divisions – bishops, clergy and laity – though it is noted by connoisseurs that the clergy are two votes short of the two-thirds majority which final approval would need. With a bigger turnout the dog-collars could yet strangle the scheme, though the country would think they were mad. Some of them are, at least, neurotic.

I walk along the river to the National Theatre where the family take me to see *Six Characters in Search of an Author*. A sombre birthday treat, it has to be said, but vastly better than standing up in a roomful of people shouting at each other, drinking bad wine and pretending to be a party. Family are a great joy and get nicer as I – and they – get older.

February 28th

Sylvia announces one of her Saturday Art Excursions and to her surprise I volunteer for the Cork Street run. It is not true that I don't care for painting: it is just that looking at painting is the most exhausting activity I know.

The Mayor Gallery has tough black charcoal drawings of Spanish cliffs by the newly 'discovered' David Bomberg. £5,000 apiece. Curiously, there are also Bomberg paintings, full of colour and much the same size, for £3,500 or less. Why the difference? I like them all but can't afford any. No doubt in ten years' time I shall tear my hair at such short-sightedness.

Across the road the Waddington empire is showing John Hoyland. Big sticky gateaux with icing sugar; yummy and *très, très* Waddington. For prices, enquire at the desk if you dare.

Finally around the British Modern Movement Show at the Royal Academy. Like all mixed exhibitions, despite careful grouping, the pictures kill each other off. I emerge with a bad case of dazzle. I hope Bomberg realises, in Heaven, that he's been discovered at last. And Paul Nash comes out of it rather well. But rather a put-down for Patrick Heron, with only one canvas. And no Terry Frost at all.

March 1st

The test of a good exhibition is: am I still thinking about it next day? I am, especially about Paul Nash. But spend the day in bed to get rid of a cold.

Up in the evening to split a bottle of champagne with George and Irene Engle who call to keep my birthday going. George, who keeps pecking away at my incomprehensible belief in God, brings me a home-made montage based on my Pisces birth-sign. It includes an extract from William Lilly's *Christian Astrology* of 1647 to the effect that when Jupiter is ill-placed I am 'Hypocritically Religious and stiffe in maintaining false Tenents in Religion; of a grosse, dull Capacity, Schismaticall, abasing himself in all Companies, crooching and stooping where no necessity is.'

With friends like these . . .

March 3rd

A sandwich lunch at the Athenaeum with me as the floor-show, addressing one of those little coteries that love to gather for intellectual self-improvement. About a score of civil servants and Whitehall fringers.

The subject: How to Beat Depression. I talk on this occasionally since, having been through the experience, I may have something helpful to say. But with reluctance. I describe the progress and treatment of my disorder, of how secret it is, how hard for the victim to confess it or for his friends to guess; of its varieties and the various treatments that have been known to work – pills, diets, electric shocks and (in my case) lying on a couch and talking to a Viennese refugee. I end up saying there is now more hope for the sufferer from depression than for the sufferer from back pains. But I believe the recovered depressive has to learn what 'triggers' to avoid if he is not to relapse. In my case they include over-work, frantic rushing to beat the clock, and the company of active depressives. Which is one reason why I dislike giving talks on the subject, because it invariably attracts them into the audience. During the discussion – which was highly intelligent and sympathetic – one member remarked that he quite understood my reluctance. He had been a local organiser of Samaritans. Two of his volunteers had been depressives who joined out of gratitude. But both were so upset by the incoming phone-calls from other depressives, they'd killed themselves.

Going down in the Athenaeum lift I remarked what a peculiar shape it was – so long and narrow. Yes, I was told: designed that way to take the coffins of members who expired in the smoking room.

March 4th

Lunch with my agent John (or is it Richard?) Parker. Fortunately I don't have to make excuses for the lateness of a manuscript and so can enjoy my *fegato* with sage while he explains the finer points of the contract for this diary which he has negotiated with Old Treacle-Voice (alias Tom Rosenthal of Deutsch – nickname courtesy of the *Guardian* diary).

Home to find the house full of elegant middle-aged print-making ladies shrieking with laughter. Truly, women's laughter is the happiest, most joyful sound in the world, untainted by the coarseness and brutality that lurks behind male ribaldry. Though it turns out that – for reasons I missed – the printmakers are laughing about gay airline stewards.

What they are *supposed* to be doing is putting together an art show at very short notice. It appears that the gallery in Pond Square, Highgate, is faced with a month of blank walls on account of its next exhibitor being carried off to hospital. The space has been offered to Sylvia who, having exhibited just before Christmas, hasn't enough left to fill the gallery on her own. So she phones round her print-making buddies and – Bingo! Instant exhibition!

One of the gang is Marianne Fox Ockinga, whose husband Robert ('Yomper') Fox of Falklands fame is put to work crossly on his word-processor churning out the invitations. I think I may escape with little more than a press handout. But oh! the uproar of framing and carting and hanging makes my heart whimper. I can hear the sound of splintering glass already. One of the advantages of the literary arts is that there's nothing to break.

March 6–9th

Suitcase time. We have not been down to Carfury since Christmas. In addition to seeing how our youngest daughter – Diana – is faring in the twenty-second week of pregnancy, we don't like to leave our cottage, the Old Sunday School, unvisited too long.

The S-registration Renault 12 is getting slightly suspect by now; but having put the two cats in their basket and the suitcases into the boot, off we go on the three hundred miles to Penzance. Sixty miles along the M4, Sylvia driving, the engine runs rough, loses power, comes to a halt beside one of the SOS telephones. Along comes AA man (looking more like a jobbing gardener) prods the distributor and says we need new HT leads. We stagger on to Hungerford and replace them. The cure lasts thirty miles. The next AA man says it is clearly the condenser, which he fits for a pittance and off we go. For another thirty miles. AA man number 3 plays about with the air intake and mutters 'compression'. After the fourth breakdown, in the sleet, beside a vandalised telephone at Taunton Dene, we decide to spend the night at Exeter and go next morning to a real garage. So we drive very carefully to Exeter – and then to Plymouth – and then all the way to Carfury. Provided it is not asked to go over fifty-five the Renault co-operates. *I* diagnose endogenous depression.

But the night is young. It is only 11 pm. We turn on the Old Sunday School's water at the mains and receive a shower-bath from the ceiling. The myth that pipes never freeze in Cornwall has burst. But comes the dawn and come obliging Cornish craftsmen (calling me *Squire*) who mend the pipes and dry out the electrical system and leave us with everything running and a bill which would not have got them out of bed in London.

Diana tears herself away from her herd of cows and drives over from Camborne with her husband Raymond.

Even the shaggiest of pullovers cannot conceal the fact that our first grandchild is on the way – but it *has* to be concealed for another six weeks, because if Diana declares herself then she'll get paid maternity leave; but if her employer finds out before that – farmers being canny with their cash – he just might dispense with her services and leave her wageless. Farm workers are still, as they've always been, the slave class of society. As chance will have it, Diana's farmer fell off his horse a few days back and is now immobilised where he can't see her; so she doesn't have to play hide and seek behind the tractor for a while. She is trying to build up a smallholding on which she can live – together with Raymond's car repair business – when she retires from being a hired herdsperson. So far it consists of a scrap of land, two horses, two dogs, one cat, six ducks and ten calves picked up cheap at auction.

Sunday is crisp and sunny. Sylvia and I walk over the burnt moors to Gurnard's Head, where we are gathered up by Phoebe Atkins and lunched at Gear, her farmhouse near-by. Phoebe's husband, Guy, was a lecturer in West African dialects at the School of Oriental and African studies and is the world expert on the Danish painter Asger Jorn. A bizarre combination, I grant you, but either would require a pretty drastic alternative by way of relief. Guy has been battered over the past few years by a series of strokes, from each of which he has risen like a bear that's been hit over the head and temporarily knocked out. Huge credit to Phoebe – we had never expected to see him on his feet again – but there he was, presiding over the table as wittily as ever in English, German and Yoruba.

Our fellow guests are hardly less exotic. There is a German painter from Cape Cornwall who came to England in 1945 as a captured Nazi commando; a fairly conventional art historian from Cambridge; and his wife who looks like a member of the Peruvian royal family in a black eye-patch, and turns out to be 50% Japanese, 25% Scottish and 25% Spanish. Racism, it appears, is not exclusively European.

The Japanese, she tells us, find it unacceptable that a person of mixed blood should speak their language perfectly as she does. The German painter contributes some shameful stories about life in an English concentration camp.

Next morning we lag the water-pipes, drain the system, and drive back eastwards in the depressive Renault. A sedate 'not over fifty-five' regime gets us back by way of Bristol, where we pick up our younger son Oliver. He and his mate Natasha have a stylish flat in a Clifton terrace, with little by way of furnishing except a mattress and an Indian *Veena* in a huge wickerwork coffin. Oliver says he is organising a cabaret to bring Bristol some much-needed night-life. Well, we shall see.

Arrive faultlessly back in Temple Fortune Lane at 6 pm. The cats are much relieved to find the central heating at work. They do not much fancy Cornwall in its cruel season.

March 10th

I knew it! I knew it! The Guild of Laughing Lady Printmakers immediately call a meeting downstairs and in next to no time I am typing press releases and *curricula vitae* for them. In other circles it is well known that typing is women's work – but not among printmakers. Printmakers take a pride in not being able to type and not allowing their daughters to learn it, either. Sylvia took a course herself at the local Adult Institute and was discharged for incompetence. So far as printmakers are concerned, typing is men's work and both Robert Fox and I are exhibited as proof.

Just manage to find time to answer fourteen letters that have piled up during our absence in Cornwall. One scolds me for making a careless joke about incest. Most of the others are invitations from worthy causes that I can only decline with guilt. So I regret that I cannot address the

Christian students of Newcastle or the Healing Circle of Truro or write an introduction to the Dean of Barchester's memoirs or become a patron of the Chastity Trust or the St Giles Home for the Hideously Deformed. The latter want me to suggest the names of very rich friends who can give them money. But I have no such friends. The former are sure I will understand that 'as a charity we cannot offer any fee but are confident you will find the experience rewarding'. But will I?

What *is* rewarding is to get a letter from a woman in Southampton who has just read the autobiography and has bits of it pinned up over her desk to give her the courage to go on living. Which makes it worthwhile.

March 11th

Life's rich tapestry has its moth-holes and gravy stains. By and large our friends are a monogamous and even monogynous lot; but how to behave towards W – already divorced from X and married to Y – when you know he's been having an affair with Z which Y has tackled head-on and routed, bringing W firmly to heel? We know this from T, U and V; but do W and Y know we know? W is insufferably brilliant and presumably in search of eternal youth, but old-fashioned words like cad and bounder rise to the lips. Can it be that Priestland is envious? No, and I resent your suggestion. Of course there are temptations if you are foolish enough to leave the door ajar to them. But honour, fidelity and – dammit – decency ought to boot them right out again the moment they show their noses. In any case, it's just too complicated, juggling an affair and a marriage simultaneously. I don't see how I could find the time or the energy to fit them both in with the other things I like to do.

Next gravy stain: four old BBC drinking companions have been given the push – something almost unheard of in the Corporation, where I always understood you had to do something *gross* – gross incompetence, gross negligence, gross indecency – to get sacked. Normal incompetence etc. were tolerated. Only recently was a chap demoted for sexual harassment (hitherto routine) and years ago a reporter was put down for running over the toe of a car-park attendant who refused to let him in ('More than my job's worth, sir . . .').

Some detect the hand of the new Director General, Michael Checkland, in the slaughter of the not-so-innocent. There is much moaning at the bar. But I fear the axe had long been hovering over the convivial quartet. There were complaints about too many liquid lunches (I was a guest at some of them), of low productivity, waning powers and dead wood. But surely the world of public relations will find homes for most of them and there's free-lancing to be had on the World Service.

Robert Fox is not one of the four. An abrasive personality, it's true, but scandalously under-used on the air, he is jumping before he is pushed. He's off to join his fellow Falklands yomper Max Hastings on the *Telegraph*. That the BBC should let a man with Robert's talents slip away like that says something to its discredit in my view. The semi-literate have spread themselves like green bay trees. Radio news is full of parochial trivialities, badly written and often unreadable. Television bulletins, like fireworks displays, are full of sound and fury, signifying very little. And that alarming Star Wars opening at nine o'clock, in which the newsreaders are bombarded with chewing-gum tablets from outer space, and hit back with bars of fudge.

A few days later: Checkland appoints one John Birt as his journalistic right-hand. Immediate outcry from (I suspect) the barbarians in power, followed by approving noises from the NCO class beneath them. In the past Birt has said and written some sensible things about the philosophy of television news, commercial though his background may be. It remains to be seen whether he realises that the key to it all is not gigantic schemes of reorganisation with more and more titles being wedged into the hierarchy, nor shovelling more technology into the studio, but keeping things as simple as possible and supporting those who have the talent to broadcast effectively. Just put John Cole on and let him tell us things.

All of which applies equally to radio news. Perhaps radio depends even more upon who is at the microphone. I hope it will be allowed to stay on its own in Portland Place and not be deported to the space centre at the White City. No businessman or politician wants to be dragged out there. Apart from anything else, there's nowhere decent for the staff to shop in the lunch hour – not an art gallery or a bookshop within walking distance.

March 15th

The Guild of Laughing Lady Printmakers open their show in Highgate. The usual mob scene with plonk and twiglets and everyone standing with their backs to the pictures, but every presence is gratefully noted. It is rather like having a preview of your own funeral . . . Oh, come now! There must be a happier comparison than that: what I'm trying to say is that a private view is when an artist tells who her real friends are – mostly other artists who can't afford to buy.

Admittedly Sylvia is fielding a second eleven of pictures left over from her November show, but I'm extremely proud of them. The others are pleasant illustrations but hers, I think, are important images in their own right and sometimes remarkably tough. Not a lot of sales, though, and if one is going to sell it is usually on the opening day.

I pick up a hint that another old friend of the WXYZ generation is feeling down in the dumps, so I charge off a little tipsily to cheer him up. Oh, the curse of being an only-child, over-achieving public schoolboy, laden with honours and wisdom but convinced that one's best can never be good enough! I know the symptoms all too well. I force a little whisky between his teeth, setting a good example myself, but I fear he is more of a puritan than I and does not enter into the spirit.

Success and happiness seldom keep company.

March 17–18th

I have to be in Padstow to be interviewed by Harry Secombe about Cornish saints. Well, it's a living. So I push my Cornish saints book into the suitcase and climb aboard the Cornish Riviera Express bound for St Austell. Having made the mistake of bringing with me a manuscript of appalling piety – submitted for my advice – there is little to do but eat; and it is an agreeably otherworldly sensation to sit there eating, while a huge turntable revolves slowly on either side displaying scenes from the English countryside.

At St Austell I hire a car – a much nicer car than the manic-depressive Renault – and drive past saint after saint: signposts indicating St Mawgan and St Issey and St Eval and St Merryn and St Mabyn and the charming St Endellion (who was very fond of cows) until I reach Padstow. A preposterously posh hotel is full up at thirty-nine quid a night, but I get a perfectly adequate room at a pub for only twelve (including a thumping breakfast). It flies the Welsh dragon over the door and is known locally as 'the Welsh Embassy', which is right and proper seeing that St Petroc, who founded the town, was a Welshman.

Padstow looks like a North Cornwall version of Mousehole, only the fishing seems busier, with several trawlers from Brixham – south coast Devon – unloading. I pay a call on St Petroc's church and find that he's usually depicted with a wolf at his feet. It's a characteristic of saints that animals feel at ease with them, and Cornish saints seem to be particularly attractive to them. Endellion's brother Nectan was a great pig man. So was Credan of Sancreed. And there was my favourite Sithney, the patron saint of mad dogs.

I do not sleep too well on account of an international euchre tournament going on at the Welsh Embassy past midnight. With the dawn, it hails. But by the time Harry Secombe's monstrous convoy arrives on the quay – generators, sound truck, mobile canteen and cars full of chief assistants to the assistant chiefs – the sun is up and twinkling on the waves. Harry hastily mimes a song about the Sea of Galilee before the tide goes out. Then we retreat for coffee into a vast American mobile home provided as his dressing room.

Secombe is a most agreeable man, a relaxed professional who does his homework, gets things right first time, doesn't throw tantrums. He's done 154 of these semi-religious Highway shows and you can tell that the crew and he like and trust one another – there's no back-biting behind the caravans. Warmed up against the wind, we perch ourselves on a bollard and chat about saints for five minutes. No second take needed, so I drive back to St Austell and reluctantly hand the car in. It seems a long way to come for five minutes' 'work', but, as I say, it pays. Poor old radio, which I actually prefer, wouldn't offer one-fifth the fee.

Still unable to face the pious manuscript I eavesdrop in the train on the way back to Paddington. Sitting in front of me are a rugger-playing young man and an extremely beautiful girl who might have stepped out of an American soap opera. Is she a model? Is she a receptionist? Is she an air hostess? Well, whatever she does for a living, the young man finds out too late that in her spare time (of which she now has six hours) she's a Jesus freak, a one-to-one evangelist, and while he wants her body all she wants is his soul. She wrestles him for it half-way across Cornwall and right across Devon, Somerset, Wiltshire and Berkshire until he whimpers for mercy and promises to take Jesus into his life. She'd have him down on his knees at 125 miles an hour, only the table is in the way. From her accent I think she *is* American and she's preaching a very American gospel: 'From the moment you start to love the Lord', she says, 'everything changes. You'll find you get job offers, that flat you want, the money you need so badly. Just ask and it shall be given – He promises that! Just look what He's done for me!' And she draws her hands indicatively across smartly tailored breasts.

March 23rd

I have been asked by the Churches' Television Centre (CTVC) to do the interviews and commentary for a film they are making about the International Year of the Homeless. The idea is to show how homeless people are trying to cope with their predicament in London, Caracas (Venezuela) and Madurai (South India). Preliminary research indicates that the Londoners come out worst.

Television is, in fact, my least favoured medium, largely because it takes eight people, half a day and several thousand pounds to record the tiniest gesture. But you can't deny it's the way to get the message to the people, and it pays extremely well, so I agree to do it.

The script calls for an opening shot of me coming home at the end of the day, trudging through the wind and rain, into comfortable home, and sinking into an armchair to contemplate how lucky I am. Net running time: twenty-five seconds. A wet, windy night obligingly turns up.

Now, I know that if there is one thing Sylvia loathes it is having a camera crew in her house. Privacy is her religion. Being an extremely modest person, whose ideal reincarnation would be as a fly on the wall, it is trying enough for her to have a husband who shamelessly makes a living by showing off in public. But to have this going on in her own home is almost more than she can bear. She claims it will entice burglars. I insist it will discourage them by showing we have nothing worth burgling. In the end the crew arrives, behaves as impeccably as boy scouts on bob-a-job day, but takes two-and-a-half hours – which is the way it goes in this cumbersome business of faking the natural. The star of the show is the Burmese cat – Mi-Nyoo – who takes her cue half a dozen times to trot across the room, jump onto my lap, and purr. Watch this space for transmission times.

March 27th

The suitcase doesn't know where it's going, and nor do I. The CTVC project which should have had me off to India tomorrow has broken down because the Indians have failed to come up with our visas. I must say I did have a suspicion from the start that CTVC were being rather optimistic: there was such a helpful man at the High Commission in London, they said. But as I know all too well, back in Delhi there is red tape, inefficiency and brooding suspicion. Why are these ex-imperialists coming to expose our backwardness? Why do they want to feature the efforts of a Christian missionary? Why must they go to Tami country where terrorists have just blown up a railway bridge? It smells like cultural espionage.

Maybe the trouble lies in nothing more sinister than an overflowing in-tray in the External Affairs ministry. There is talk of going to Africa – to Lusaka – instead, which I find less appealing. Wherever it is, my diary is disrupted, time wasted, people disappointed. Sylvia's friends have laid on lots of little parties and outings to comfort her in my absence: now I shan't be absent at all, but skulking in the shadows undergoing the abandonment myself.

We did film (or rather videotape) some London homelessness, around the bed and breakfast hotels in King's Cross where the boroughs park women with small children. Apart from anything else, it does not make sense economically: a council flat might cost the social services £70 a week – B & B costs at least £300 a week for one room, minimal facilities, a tea-and-toast breakfast. But the hoteliers get fat on block bookings: my researcher says one gets a million a year from a single borough (which spends seventeen millions a year on its B & B clients).

Julian, the researcher, does the dirty work of digging up victims for me to interview, and I'm grateful to him for taking the edge off the embarrassment that way and for finding me some fairly spirited and articulate specimens. One is an attractive Ethiopian lady with an eighteen-month-old son. She is a stateless refugee anyway – I suspect her family was too aristocratic for the Derg's liking – but she did once have a home in Harrogate until four well-dressed British fascists came along and informed her that according to the Bible she was sub-human and not wanted in the neighbourhood. While she was at church, somebody wrecked the house and spattered the baby's cot with blood-red paint – so she took the first train to London and threw herself on the mercy of Camden. In her case – as in most I come across – there's a family breakdown involved. 'Husbands' walk out, fathers acquire new 'wives', mothers kick nubile daughters onto the streets or make life intolerable for jobless sons. There seems to be a steady drain of hopeless cases out of Scotland.

A huge gale blows up during Thursday night. On Friday morning Ken Wood (our policeman neighbour at Carfury) rings up to say it's peeling slates off the Sunday School roof; so I beg him to get the builder down the lane to administer first aid. Fortunately Oliver and Tasha are driving down there from Bristol this afternoon; but they had better lash themselves down when they arrive.

April 2nd

Our eldest child, Jennet – who is thirty-six, a graphic designer and a great beauty – drops in after her six-monthly check-up at the Royal Free Hospital. It is bad news. The cancer (Hodgkin's Disease) which was driven out of her five years ago is back – no point in asking why, it just is. The hospital say they will be able to blast it out of her again, but we all know the dreadful ordeal that lies ahead, the repeated poisoning with chemicals and roasting with radiation. Still, the Priestlands will rally round as they did before and command the evil spirit to come out of her. It shan't have her – she's ours.

We tell her that with some vehemence. But after she's gone, we droop. 'Oh, not again!' groans Sylvia. 'It's like an old pain that you'd managed to forget coming back – and all of a sudden you remember it all too well.' Dear Sylvia: she never stops being a mother to her children, night or day, however old they may think they are.

The Churches' Television people say that 'permission for filming the work of Brother James Kimpton in South India has not been granted' though we have been assured that this will not affect any future visa application. In other words, it is a local anti-Christian hate and not an objection to me personally. Which is something of a relief in case I want to visit India in the future.

Instead we are going to Lusaka, Zambia, on May 1st. Meanwhile the Quaker centre at Pendle Hill, Pennsylvania, where Sylvia and I are due to take up residence for a term in September, writes chirpily to say it plans to send us on tour as far afield as Oregon. Jennet rings up to say we must on no account alter any plans because of her illness. We say of course not; but we shall tear up everything, in fact, if it is necessary to be with her.

Spring seems to be taking a grip on things at last. Blossom. Bullfinches. Daffodils. Etcetera. But I do not feel much like cheering.

April 3rd

What a chronicle of sorrows this is becoming! I rattle down to Eastbourne to deliver the eulogy at the cremation of my mentor Palmer ('Ritz') Ritzema, who taught me how to write for radio when I joined BBC News back in the early 1950s. He died quite quickly of a lung cancer, aged seventy-five, at which one can't really grumble.

It takes a good man's funeral to resurrect old friends these days. There are six or eight members of the Ritz family in the chapel and a dozen retired BBC colleagues in their sixties, seventies, with Teddy Thompson, the old parliamentary correspondent, in his eighties and very spry with it. In the train going back Teddy lectures us in detail on the Shakespearean quartos and folios. Bidding each other goodbye at Victoria someone remarks 'Well, I dare say we shall be meeting again before long at one crematorium or another . . .'

Ritz really was a good man: unambitious, one of nature's Quakers, a conscientious objector during World War Two when the BBC was required to sack all 'conchies' however useful they might have been to it. To its credit, the Corporation reinstated him within weeks of the War's end. Thank Heaven it was not the First World War when the official state policy was to terrorise conchies into giving up; but it was still a lonely row to hoe – literally, for they put Ritz on the land. I think the experience gave Ritz's outward gentleness its inner strength. Towards the end of his BBC career they put him in charge of a properly organised training scheme for young journalists. It was the ideal job for him, for he revered the language and believed in and passed on a quality of spoken journalism now – alas – out of fashion. And somebody once called him 'the conscience of the newsroom'.

Before the coffin rumbles off down the conveyor belt to the furnace, I can't help recalling that when we first met I was supposed to be writing the formal obituaries which the BBC broadcast when distinguished persons handed in their dinner pails – that is, approved and carefully graded distinguished persons. And now, here I am delivering Ritz's. How he must be chortling. 'I say, young Gerry, don't go overdoing it! Even cabinet ministers are only allowed two minutes and fifteen seconds! You're giving me an over-run!'

April 4th

To the Royal Academy for the exhibition of Greek icons. They should have provided room for one to worship and fall down before them – put incense in the air conditioning – lit the show with honey-scented beeswax candles. *Kyrie eleison, Christe eleison, Kyrie eleison.*

Of course a lot of the saints and apostles are just symbolic representations. But some – Peter, Paul, Nicholas, Christ himself – are so much more that I can't resist the eerie feeling they really did look like this, that the tradition has not erred. But I am not so convinced by the Virgin, I'm afraid. A child remarks: 'Mummy, all the ladies have babies; and all the men gold hats.'

April 5th

A Sunday, but I totter into Broadcasting House early to be interviewed about the alleged disgraceful behaviour of 'the media' at the loss of the channel ferry *Herald of Free Enterprise* off Zeebrugge. This is supposed to be a religious programme, though I do not quite see the religious significance of the item. Morality and religion may be relatives, but not identical twins. Anyhow, I say my bit about the need for journalists to assert their consciences and occasionally refuse to commit a public nuisance; and then I head for the exit. Where I meet an old BBC hack on his way to the newsroom. 'Just heard you on the car radio,' he says, 'and I quite agree about refusing to do stories on moral grounds. Only I did that at Radio Solent a few years ago – and they sacked me.'

April 6th

The Priestland Postal Clinic for Depressives has to reopen. A desperate letter arrives from a senior police officer in Wales. Six months ago his mother died and now he is plunged into darkness and thinking of killing himself. His GP has doped him up to his back teeth with four different drugs, but it only makes him feel physically as well as mentally ill. And he is spiritually ill too because, as a 'low-profile Christian', he is ashamed that he can't *pray* himself better. But someone has sent him some photocopied pages of my autobiography in which I describe my own sufferings and recovery: he knows that part of my regime is to avoid the company of other depressives: but PLEASE (his capitals) can I help?

I write back along the usual lines: I am totally unqualified as a psychiatrist – I know there are varieties of depression and varieties of treatment appropriate to each – but I'm in no position to prescribe for his case. Nevertheless there is hope – I've known many recoveries, though none due to prayer or 'pulling yourself together'. It sounds to me as if he needs to talk, talk, talk uninhibitedly, which must be difficult for a man in his position. Of course it's easier for him to be frank with invisible me than with his own doctor – but he must open up with him, let it all come out, and beg to be referred to a consultant psychiatrist. The guy is obviously so choked with guilt over his mother's death and shame at his own weakness that he's in a constant flood of tears; but nowadays there's no reason to be ashamed. Talk, goddamit, as frankly as you write.

I just hope the letter gets there in time. His appeal was forwarded to me through the BBC, which has meant a delay.

April 8th

A somewhat disappointing cheque from my agent . . . On the other hand *The Sunday Times* commissions a piece about Easter ('believing in Christianity is like riding a bicycle,' I carol. 'It's an unlikely thing to work anyway, and if you lose faith it falls over . . . There's quite an industry now of non-cyclists explaining why the bicycle can't work . . . it reminds one of the "Who *really* killed President Kennedy?" school of literature'). There is said to be a glimmer of hope that Jennet's trouble may not be malignant after all. Friday night is *Simone Boccanegra* night at the Coliseum. My depressive Welsh policeman writes to say he has made an appointment to see a psychiatrist and is now full of hope. And on Monday we're off to Cornwall for ten days, so let us cheer up.

Morale is certainly lifted by dinner shared with Mary Edmond and Annetta Hoffnung. Sylvia does a super soup of jade-green spinach, followed by a well-dressed *osso bucco* and then cheese. The company of three elegant and intelligent women is extremely agreeable: no competitive male posturing or splitting up into little cliques. Mary has just finished a book about William Davenant, the Stuart playwright, impresario and gun-runner who claimed to be Shakespeare's godson (and possibly even closer). Annetta is still trying to get through a biography of her husband Gerard who died (how the years scamper) twenty-eight years ago. Towards the end of the evening she tells, in her little flower-like voice, a story worthy of Gerard's own taste in *grand guignol*:

There was this man who kept a python as a pet. One night he falls asleep watching the television, an arm hanging loose by his side, and wakes up with a feeling of tightness round the arm and a burning sensation in his hand. Looking down he sees the python has swallowed his arm up to the elbow and has started to digest the hand. Impossible to pull the creature off because its teeth are locked, so with his free hand he rings for the vet who has to come and kill the snake and . . . Are you still with me?

April 12th

Michael Duffy is headmaster of King Edward VI School at Morpeth in Northumberland and the sort of man I find it hard to say no to, on account of a certain magnetism or charisma I suppose. He has commanded me to give the sermon at the annual conference service of the Secondary Heads Association, of which he is president this year. So I go up to Nottingham – one of the better conference universities thanks to Jesse Boots's money. Some of the newer universities are more like pharmaceutical factories or enlightened reformatories, but Nottingham has a certain stateliness like the government complex of a nation about the size of New Zealand.

There are 250 heads being put together – mostly head-masters with just a sprinkling of headmistresses including some jolly nuns. *En masse* you couldn't guess what they were – the essential solitariness of the head cannot survive multiplication. But catch one alone in a corner or striding across a lawn by himself, and he's instantly a head again.

I preached on 'The Word of God and the words of man' – how it's only when we shut up and stop trying to tell Him who He is that He has a chance to make Himself heard. Michael let me choose the hymns, promising lusty singing, so I had 'Thou whose almighty word' to Moscow to propel me into the pulpit; and 'Lord, Thy word abideth' to Ravenshaw to get me out. The heads, accustomed to leading reluctant assemblies every morning, sang with vigour and feeling and by the end of it I was almost in tears. That strange, rare tingling came over me and made me fearful that one day I shall come to and be told I have been speaking in Aramaic. Watch out! Watch out! There's a Paraclete about!

April 13–20th

And so to Carfury – where nothing has been done about the gale damage to the roof, the local builder arguing that since the rain wasn't coming through he could devote his energies to more urgent cases – of which there is much evidence. Every other roof in the landscape has its first-aid patch of fertiliser bags and turf.

The drive down was (this time) uneventful. Instead of the senile Renault we drove the uncomfortable but reliable Ford Escort whose insides are little more complex than those of a motor mower.

Sylvia is right in saying that if we moved permanently to Carfury (which the romantic side of me would love to do) not only would we lose the London market-place where both of us sell most of our work – we would lose the contrast. And it is contrast that keeps the imagination on its toes. Up in London, you can slog through the same timetable any day of the year, whatever the weather. Down in Cornwall not only does one sleep longer (negative ions in the maritime air, perhaps) but paces oneself according to the light, the tides, the season. It exercises animal instincts one ignores up-country.

Our younger daughter Diana is cheerfully pregnant. B-day is expected early in July. After years of slave labour for her farmer she has given in her notice and decided not to go back. She hopes to make ends meet, on top of Raymond's car-mending business, by buying and selling calves which she will raise on odd scraps of land she manages to rent. Six of the little creatures are now parked on the half acre behind our Old Sunday School, and they immediately become the most counted cattle in Penwith.

Which is just as well, because on our second morning there isn't a single calf in sight. They've slipped out through some slack barbed wire. My mind full of bloody images of calves on the A30, I drive around in vain; until a helpful neighbour advises me that cows always seek their own kind and the best thing is to rummage through all the local herds. Which Sylvia and I do, stumbling on foot through the jigsaw puzzle of fields between Trythall and Ding Dong, until at last we discover our runaways among a rabble destined for execution at the Madron slaughterhouse. During the next two hours we learn a lifetime's experience of cow body-language, cow tactics and strategy, cow mind-reading, cow anticipation. It is like being the dogs in one of the BBC's shepherd trials. And just as Diana arrives with her trained cow-dog Kallee (who could have done the job in five min-utes) we have achieved the 'fetch', the 'shedding' and even the final 'pen'. It was actually rather fun; a refreshing change from doing a thousand words for *The Sunday Times* on the Resurrection Today. See what I mean about contrast?

Saturday brings another uniquely Penwith experience. Diana and Raymond are going to a farm auction to pick up a few cheap items for the calf ranch. They do it very cannily, deciding in advance what they want and what their limit is, never allowing themselves to be provoked into a battle which will leave them with a seven-pound bill when they only meant to pay five. Since Diana is altogether too emotional to be trusted with the bidding, Raymond signals with tiny twitches of the eyebrows and comes away with three electric fence transformers: exactly what the Sunday

School calves need, and not a penny over the budget. If only I had such self-control. Though I must say I was at a loss to work up much desire for 98% of what was on offer.

Cars, trailers and pickups come bouncing in from Morvah and Relubbus, Cripplesease, Mulfra and Splattenridden – the parking lot looks like a point-to-point meeting. Next to it the selling field is laid out with row upon row of lots which look as if they have been dragged out of nettlebeds – heaps of third-hand corrugated iron, piles of broken cinder-blocks, glass with no window-frames, window-frames with no glass – lots and lots of lots and lots and lots.

The market consists mainly of Penwith's middle peasantry – the cloth-cap-wearing class: a layer of society undreamed of in Hampstead Garden Suburb. Male to a man, they trudge after the auctioneer with the stoicism of a herd of steers looking for the one sound turnip in a heap of rotters. Some of them – wild men from the moors with greasy locks matted with greasy beards – look as if they sleep under bushes, but drive away with their purchases in Land Rovers. Others seem to have been moulded in one piece from their boots to their cloth caps, so that it is impossible to imagine them in the nude or even indoors. Their very movements, evolved for progress through mud and furrows, must make them like fish out of water in their wives' TV lounges.

We trudge our way despondently past heap after heap, the auctioneer (who resembles the rest, except that he is bare-headed and waves a cane) crying, 'Come now gennelmen – got to be five poun' for this lot!' But, no thank you, it hasn't. 'Poun' note, then? Two! It's with the pipe – against the 'at!' The owners of the pipe and hat turn their backs and slouch away, leaving someone else to pay three pounds for two inscrutable bits of metal. There is always somebody who will buy *anything*. Whether he is in the pay of the auctioneer or the agent of some ultimate market which stops the bottom dropping out of rubbish, I do not know; but at this particular sale nothing is unsellable, even if it has to be cast in with the lot following, so that in order to get two deck chairs (lot 167) you have to accept lot 166 (three toilet cisterns 'said to be in working order though as you know this does not constitute my guarantee, gennelmen').

Agriculture has its own iconography. Pieces of rusty iron which mean nothing to you or me assume enormous significance in the eyes of the devotee of this or that particular tractor-system. Thus a pair of metal rods may fetch eight or nine pounds, while two pitchforks, three rakes and five shovels are shrugged off for a wunner. Chains – if they are big, fat chains with ingenious hooks and swivels – are worth their weight in gold; but five yards of delicate links with no specific purpose can hardly be given away. An anvil – such as they haven't made since the first night of Wagner's *Ring* – creates a great stir and zooms up to a sky-high twenty-nine quid. Raymond and Diana regretfully see a round feeder – a vast iron coronet which might have been exhibited in some museum of modern art – go for fifty. They had fixed their limit at forty-five and not a penny more.

Easter Sunday we go to church in Zennor, where the vicar Shane Cotter (surely the original of half El Greco's saints) conducts what seems to me a quite irregular but wholly appropriate family service of his own concoction. It lasts only half an hour so that mothers with small children can just about get through it, though towards the end the tinies commence a pagan ritual of their own, gibbering and gesturing at one another and brandishing teddy-bears in the air. Zennor, which a dozen years ago seemed to be dying out, now has sixty children in the parish; rural depopulation has been reversed – though goodness knows how people make a living. Some, I think, have come to the conclusion that there's no point in seeking non-existent jobs up-country and if you've got to live off the DHSS you might as well do so in pleasant surroundings where you can take advantage of the sharing, bartering, favour-swapping country way of life.

I had a strange dream one night – unusually vivid. I was walking through a square which I knew to be in London although it looked much more like the Piazza Navona in Rome, with cobbles under foot. Outside a bank in one corner I saw two large cars like vintage Rollses and understood at once that there was a raid going on. Two men with long rifles came out of the bank and began shooting. Their fire was instantly returned by plain-clothes agents with machine-guns – bullets and people were flying everywhere. I lay down beside a parked car but raised myself on my elbows to see what was going on, sure that I would not be hit in spite of the fusillade that was cutting down people all around me. Then, anxious to make my way to the BBC and do an eyewitness report, I stumbled out of the square into what seemed to be the Euston Road, beside which I encountered the living statue of a male mermaid or triton – ivory-coloured, long-haired, fish-tailed – which was proclaiming, 'Regret I shall have to excommunicate those two priests . . .' I hovered for a moment between staying in the dream and waking up, but decided to wake so that I could tell the dream to myself over again and thus remember it, which I have done. I cannot see anything prophetic or symbolic in it now: just a jumble of things recently heard or read – part news, part fairy-tale, part *Church Times*.

April 26th

The last few days in Carfury are marred by a nasty bronchial cough. I often get one about this time of year, probably brought on by an allergy to pollen.

This Sunday, however, I am well enough to go to Oxford, where Geoffrey Warnock's chaplain at Hertford has snared me into preaching. So we do the round of our collection of Oxford knights and ladies: Mosers at Wadham, Bannisters at Pembroke, the Warnocks at Hertford (with the

Baroness weekending from Girton). Sylvia and I speak to hardly a commoner all day. I can't say I want a title, but I wouldn't mind a college of my own with mullioned lodgings and a walled garden and fellows who kept themselves to themselves and regarded me as a distinguished ornament to add to their row of portraits. Peevishly, perhaps, I preach on the fleetingness of fame, using as my text 'Thou fool, this night thy soul shall be required of thee . . .' The Warnocks take it very well.

May 1st

Suddenly realise I am going to Zambia today to make that film. So I fling some hot-weather type clothes into the suitcase, plus the little short-wave radio and some paperbacks, and rendezvous at Gatwick with Martin Smith, the director, and Ros Cook the unit manager, and off we fly into the night – it's the usual bus ride, there's no glamour left in flying, however hard the airline TV commercials try to pretend there is. But I have found a valuable new addition to the survival kit: a small inflatable pillow that fits round your neck like a collar and stops your head flopping about when you fall asleep. Highly recommended.

May 2nd

I seem to be in Zambia – a place few people can ever have expected to be in, even when it was called Northern Rhodesia – but here it is, lots of it, rolling red earth dotted with trees and roofed over with a pale blue dome which lets in the clear, clean light.

The natives appear to be friendly, if rather solemn, though at the moment they are a little jumpy. The South African equivalent of the SAS shot up the border town of Livingstone the other day on the excuse that it was harbouring guerrillas of the African National Congress, which it probably was. Like the Israelis, the South Africans like to keep their neighbours off balance, just in case. There is nothing much the Zambians can do in return, so they respond with the standard gesture of setting up road-blocks and examining papers, particularly those of wandering white persons with cameras round their necks. There doesn't seem to be much you can legally photograph in Zambia – certainly not post offices, bridges, electricity sub-stations or any scene with a soldier in it – so maybe it was just as well I had my little camera whipped out of my jacket by a highly skilled pick-pocket within hours of arriving. I should have known the gang was closing in for the kill when one of them started dancing to and fro in front of me waving a blue plastic bag. The moment I peered into it, his partner must have made the dip and passed the camera on, but I never felt it go. This was in Cairo Street, which passes for Lusaka's shopping centre though there is very little in the shops. Lusaka in general is rather less exciting than Billings, Montana.

Martin and Ros, meanwhile, are punching out the telephone numbers of the contacts given us in London. To little effect, at first, not only because it is a weekend but also because very few calls get connected and when they are nobody answers. When we finally penetrate the right ministry, our applications for permission to film have been lost, of course, and everything has to begin from scratch.

The only way to pass the time is to visit the Lusaka botanical gardens where, perhaps as a further security measure, none of the trees are named; and the zoo. This is a dusty concentration camp exhibiting two hot bears, two bored lions, a hyena and three sinister crocodiles with an alarming number of young. And a chimpanzee on a chain being teased to distraction by Zambian children.

Within two days I have read all my paperbacks and there appear to be no bookshops in Lusaka. The news-stand in our

31

hotel offers nothing but dust, and a neighbouring hotel has two shelves of pulp of such abysmal quality that it takes me half an hour to find a couple I can face. One is an Arthur C. Clarke which vanishes, agreeably enough, in an evening; the other is an Alistair Maclean so badly written that I wonder if it can have been pirated in Mozambique by an unemployed agency stringer. The characters' motives are inscrutable even when explained, cliché after cliché rises gratefully to its cue, men 'literally explode with anger', women bite their lips as the colour drains from their faces and their bosoms heave with barely suppressed emotion . . . O God, O Montreal!

It is enough to drive one into the Casino which is attached to our hotel and patronised by the cream of Zambian yuppidom. Actually, it is not very sinful because the stake limits are so low, the minimum on the roulette wheel being 15p and the maximum about £4, though the stacks of plastic chips being pushed across the tables make it look like millions. Even so, for me the prospect of winning is too dreadful to contemplate because it is all conducted in non-convertible Zambian *kwatchas*.

The kwatcha has become an unexpected embarrassment. When we arrived at the airport I changed some sterling at the rate of thirty-four kwatchas to the pound. But overnight – fed up with being pushed around by the International Monetary Fund – President Kaunda, whose face appears on every kwatcha note, decided the rate was an outrage and decreed thirteen to the pound with no change in local prices. So now I have far more kwatchas than I know what to do with. Normally there's drink, but the local beer, known as Mosi beer, which is light and excellent, is only K4 a bottle. Down in the depths of the hotel I discover a glum little jeweller making bangles from green malachite, so I can see it's going to be malachite bangles all round for my women-folk.

We are staying at the inevitable Intercontinental which is like Intercontinentals the world over (except that this one makes Manhattan cocktails of a unique and medicinal nastiness). I suppose if you are a travelling salesman you are grateful for the hygiene, the airconditioning and the efficient telephone system (note: the latter does not apply to the *Lusaka* Intercontinental). But it is extra-terrestrial living of a kind that has nothing whatever to do with the country concerned. Wherever you are it is always Minneapolis. The amazing thing is that the natives, instead of burning the place down as an affront to their national pride, queue up and dress up to get into it. Our Intercontinental is full of Zambians in smart European suits, many of them being wined and dined by rather less smartly dressed Europeans. Every lunchtime the hotel driveway is jammed with official Range Rovers bringing ministers and party bigwigs for refreshment.

May 5th

At last we are breaking through on the bureaucratic front just as the three technicians of the crew arrive: David the cameraman, Malcolm the soundman and Stuart the electrician. They represent the modern, civilised school of film-making (actually they make electronic videotape), considerably more couth than the crews of yesteryear which left trails of destruction and ill-will wherever they went. I knew one which made up its own marching song:

A terrible thing is a camera crew;
There's 'orrible things that a crew can do.
So lock up your wives and lock up your girls
And lock up your money, your whisky, your pearls!
We'll trample your gardens and blow all your fuses!
Oh – 'ideous creatures are camera crewses!

But not this one. They are all perfect gentlemen and I find that among the six of us there are three vegetarians and three opera-lovers, no womanisers and none

33

(apart from me) who has thought to load up with duty-free spirits.

Now equipped with government press passes and a Zambian escort named Austin, we set out to film our story. Which is roughly as follows:

The colonial pattern of urban housing was that the house came with the job. Civil servants got government housing, workers got company housing, and there was bank housing, railway housing and so forth, with an underlying structure of racial and social apartheid. But with independence people started coming in from the countryside in greater numbers to seek their fortunes from the spin-off of development. Many of them settled in unofficial shanty colonies on the edge of the city. At first the reaction of government was to take a bulldozer to them; but squatters had the ingenious idea of running up the flag of the United National Independence Party (UNIP) and protesting that as loyal branches of the one-party state it would be unthinkable to evict them.

Enlightenment prevailed. The authorities calculated that if the squatters were granted valid title to their squats, plus aid towards making the structures permanent, they would have the incentive to upgrade them from shanties into reasonable habitations, to the general benefit of society. Taking this a step further forward, the authorities would even provide 'site and services' – that is, the ground, water, electricity and drains – and the materials with which incomers could build their own homes to an approved standard. The results are not exactly luxury, but compare favourably with what I have seen in India at the same social levels. Every weekend you see people busily moulding their own concrete blocks and adding rooms onto their bungalows under the supervision of foremen from the local council which is virtually identical with the local party branch. I didn't get the impression that UNIP was a Marxist tyranny, though no doubt it has its favourites and its perqs.

The only trouble is that Zambia is just about broke. The bottom has fallen out of the copper market, the South Africans have got the economy at their mercy, and when the International Monetary Fund came in to sort things out their idea of balancing the budget was to cut subsidies and float the kwatcha until there were riots in the market-place. President Kaunda (alias Comrade Kaunda or KK in the local press) has been trying to write his way out of this by decree; but as things are at the moment, a lot of would-be self-builders are being told, 'Sorry – no grants available, you'll have to buy your own cement.'

Austin takes us round half a dozen estates, carefully signalling our arrival so that the party committee-men can put on their jackets and ties and get into the picture. But not even they can discipline the hordes of ragged urchins who leap up and down in front of the camera, waving and yelling. In the end one of the crew has to be detached as a decoy, pretending to take photographs of them with a stills camera while the video tip-toes off in another direction. In one settlement we are trapped in the minibus by a hail storm which beats on the roof with such ferocity we cannot hear ourselves speak. We could see it coming from miles away, but the Zambians told us not to be silly – it *never* rains in May.

By and large we manage to avoid politics. Just once there's an outburst from Austin who says he has heard that the British government has blamed Zambia for spreading AIDS and that we shall all have to report for AIDS testing when we get back to Britain. What about the Americans with their hundreds of thousands of cases? he demands. Zambia's got hardly any. He suspects racism. I tell him sternly there are far too many unsubstantiated rumours flying about Lusaka and that nobody's going to test us when we get home, but I am sure he doesn't believe me.

On our last day we tell Austin we need some music for our film. The hotel band plays an endless loop of Strangers in the Night, I Did It My Way, Volare and The Girl from

Ipanema; so could he get us into a Zambian night-club? After dismissing two or three names with a shudder he says the Masiye Traditional Disco might do and, golly, it does. It's a bit like an African version of the Miners' Welfare, full of men drinking bottled Mosi 'by the neck', and a band of three shockingly amplified guitars and a drummer whose daytime job must be breaking stones.

But halfway into their first rowdy number they are joined by a line of six chubby girls in white tennis skirts and pink bodices who put on an exhibition of tribal bumping and grinding for which Soho, I think, is not yet ready. What they do with their feet is banal and what they do with their arms routine; but what happens to their bellies and bottoms would drive a synod of bishops into a frenzy. It certainly inflames the customers, for the sturdiest girl has to break off from time to time to throw interlopers off the platform.

David the Camera – towing Malcolm the Sound by his umbilical – crawls round the stage after the girls, zooming in on the action while I wonder how I am going to write this into a script about housing the homeless. The only thing that spoils the evening is when we leave the club and find our minibus blocked in the car park by a Land Rover. This turns out to belong to a well-known secret policeman and nobody dares ask him to move it.

We get to bed late and I am wakened too soon by a chorus of vigorous barking. It is the truck from the security company that goes round every evening depositing a dog and its handler at each embassy in town, picking them up again at dawn. My room faces the Japanese mission, whose regular dog is either much loved or much hated by his fellows: whichever it is, they let him know it both times.

A little later the *Zambia Daily Mail* slides under the door with its usual lead story about the sinister attempts of the International Monetary Fund to undermine the Zambian economy. I'll say one thing for the *Mail* – it has a lively correspondent in Kitwe. One morning he quotes the High Court Commissioner there as earnestly advising jealous husbands 'to divorce their wives instead of beating them to death. Sentencing one such wife-slayer to eighteen months in jail, the Commissioner observed that there were other ways of solving problems than causing bodily harm to the one in the wrong.'

Another day, Our Man in Kitwe has the utterly fascinating story of the Witchdoctor Who Cheated. Fwemba 'a mobile medicine-man who wore imported suits and expensive shoes', approached a certain Malesu who was still grieving for his daughter Samba who had died two years earlier. 'I can bring your daughter back to life,' promised Fwemba, 'for she is really working on an invisible farm owned by the wealthy Chinondo. She is married to another invisible worker there. But for you – only one hundred pounds to bring her back.'

So Malesu gladly paid up and together with Fwemba and a group of elderly cronies, drove out to the site of the invisible farm. Chinondo had gone into town to buy powder for his muzzle-loading gun, so the coast was clear. Fwemba opened the front door of the Land Rover on the passenger's side, waited a moment, and assured the party that Samba had just climbed aboard and no one must sit next to the driver. She would become visible in two or three days provided the correct ceremonies were performed.

The ceremonies amounted to a prolonged feast with much music, dancing, food and Mosi. From time to time generous helpings were carried into the hut where the invisible Samba was re-materialising, and sure enough the plates came out clean and the beer-bottles empty.

On the second day Malesu was permitted a peep into the hut where a female form could be seen lying under a white cloth. 'Only she mustn't speak,' warned Fwemba, 'or the whole process could go into reverse.' Renewed dancing and feasting broke out and the District Commissioner –

described by Our Man as 'sharp-nosed and frog-eyed' – came to call. He left paying tribute to Fwemba's powers. In de-colonialised Zambia (he intimated) indigenous medicine was now treated with proper respect. In next to no time large numbers of eminent persons were turning up, stepping on one another and 'reading out long boring speeches'.

After five days of unbroken celebrations, Samba was still under the cloth making no comment. Unfortunately patience ran out before the beer did and there were rowdy scenes when the veil dropped and Fwemba and his all-too-visible accomplice were carted off by the police. Leaving the District Commissioner, no doubt, more frog-eyed than ever.

It's those long boring speeches that ring so true.

And so back to London. Kindly, the airline promotes me to first class where I discover that it *is* possible for even me to get adequate legroom, but not at the normal fare. If I were an animal I'm sure economy class would be contrary to the veterinary regulations.

May 10th

I arrive home about eight in the morning – laden with offerings of malachite – to find I am all in the wrong context. While I have been away hopes for Jennet have risen and fallen again and it is now certain she will have to undergo another six months of chemical poisoning to get the Hodgkins out of her. I am tired and upset, drink too much, am in disgrace . . . Not surprisingly, nobody wants to hear about Zambia.

May 14th

Our wedding anniversary. We have survived thirty-eight years and, trite though it may sound, it does not feel more than eighteen. I wait till Sylvia goes off teaching

one of her geriatric art classes and then buy an extravagant bunch of spiky Japanese chrysanthemums, which I
leave on the table with a 'Happy Anniversary!' note
before fleeing to somewhere in Devon. Arrow Books,
who are to publish the paperback of my autobiography,
are holding their annual salesmen's conference in a lavish
hotel near Totnes. I and three other authors are to be
the floor show. One has done a book about slimming,
one has done a walk with a dog, the third is Malcolm
Bradbury who has written the book I meant to write
some day about a sleazy imaginary people's republic (not
Zambia). The star of the occasion is, inevitably, the dog.
Authors, like actors, should never try to compete with
animals or children.

Nor is it really fair to have to compete with Bradbury,
who is the perfect literary don – witty, pipe-smoking,
MacNeicean good looks, irresistible to the swooning
young ladies who staff publishers' offices. But at least my
after-dinner speech is (I pride myself) a glass or two
less fluid than his after-dinner speech. The dog is not
asked to speak and howls all night in its master's room.

Dawn reveals a lush valley dipping down to the sea
and rich energetic people playing tennis and golf all
over the place. I eat a commercial traveller's breakfast
of eggs, bacon, sausage, black pudding, tomato and
mushrooms before being loaded onto the train back
to Paddington. Goodness knows what good this will
do for my book, or for Arrow, but I find it best to
do everything publishers ask me to do, on the grounds
that if it doesn't sell they can't blame me for not being
cooperative. The publishers' ladies insist that it makes *all*
the difference, by which I suppose they mean that it
makes a book seem alive instead of just a dead thing
sleeping on a shelf.

Get home to find the flowers a success.

May 15–16th

Becomes a Turner weekend. Sylvia develops a hankering to drive down to Petworth House, which we achieve without getting lost or jammed on the highway, and then, flashing the complimentary card which the National Trust kindly sends me every year, we enter obsequiously via the servants' quarters. In its heyday the place must have employed most of the village: think of all those fires, cans of water up and down the stairs, so many servants they must have had servants to service them. And then the outdoor staff to keep the enormous parklands in order.

It can't have been very snug as a home. In fact it is rather gloomy. But I suspect that, as at Kedleston near Derby, the family did not actually live in the grand apartments but had something cosier round at the back. The salons and galleries were there to express the family's wealth, influence and good taste, and at Kedleston anyway the public was always welcome to walk round and be impressed by it. I doubt if the muddy-booted peasantry were admitted, but even in the eighteenth century ladies and gentlemen could drive up and ask to see round the apartments much as they do today.

Petworth furnished Turner with a studio to work in; but his patron didn't necessarily buy everything he offered and J.M.W.T. often had to pipe the tune that was ordered. 'Not enough happening in that left-hand corner,' commented His Lordship of one sublime parkscape. So Turner had to put a cricket match in amongst the browsing deer, though he made it a rather ghostly affair.

Lots more Turners to be seen in the new Clore Galleries at the Tate, though I still think they would have been happier in Somerset House. The architect, Stirling, has scaled the thing pretty well from the outside, though the entrance is rather too deliberate an attempt to call attention to its own modernity, and the foyer suggests you are entering a secure psychiatric hospital. Fortunately you can't see it much from the road. Sylvia is scathing about the reflecting pool, whose waterlilies have, of course, been immediately killed off by acid rain and cigarette ends. But she cheers up on discovering that a wild duck and drake have taken up residence.

Inside it's all very padded, sealed-up and obsessive, as if a dangerous lunatic were confined there. I dare say that is how some people *did* see Turner, but I still think the pictures would gain – as they do at Petworth – from one's being able to contrast them from time to time with the real world glimpsed through a window. There's only one window accessible to the public in the Clore, and people were queueing up to get at it.

But what a man – what a musician of paint – Turner was! Grabbing handfuls of sea and light and clouds and turning a fleeting moment into a symphony. A great journalist, too, always trying to convey that essential feeling of *what it was like* – and so laying himself open to the charge of sensationalism.

May 18th

Without much hesitation we have made the decision: now that we know Jennet has to undergo another, harrowing course of chemical therapy for Hodgkin's Disease, we can't push off for three months to the United States in the Autumn. I have this offer of a term as Visiting Friend-in-Residence at the Quaker study centre called Pendle Hill near Philadelphia; and it would enable me to do the American research that I need for my book on the Quaker Movement. But we know from the experience of five years ago that Jennet will need all the family support she can get during her ordeal. It will drive her almost – though not quite (they are very skilful at it) – out of her mind. And it will do much the same, at a less deadly level, to Sylvia if we aren't there to minister with everything from grapes to sympathy.

I could not go off to Philadelphia alone, leaving Sylvia without support. So let us stop trying to juggle priorities and put the family first. We are not available for America until Jennet's treatment is over and we can concentrate our minds on other things. I write off to the American Quakers, and to the English Quaker foundation which had kindly volunteered to help with our travel expenses, asking if we can postpone the adventure. Dear Friends – they write back with understanding, sympathy, generous cooperation. Well, maybe we shall find, when the time comes and we look back, that we could have gone after all. But I would rather make a clear-cut decision now than dodge about till the last moment. The suitcase heaves a sigh of relief, but it needn't think it can slumber from now till next year. There are still plenty of bookings for it in the diary.

May 19th

I am just beginning to catch up with the fact that, after so much speculation, there really will be General Elections on June 11th. Some months ago I casually put my name to an appeal for *tactical voting* – the notion that whether they loved each other or not, Labour and Alliance ought to put their votes together where they had a chance of getting the odious Mrs Thatcher out. And now the fist has to be put where the mouth has been. This is a little embarrassing because the BBC promptly rings me up and asks if I will do the election-time Thoughts for the Day, intended to inspire the nation towards voting nobly without saying exactly how. But I have promised to go down to Bath and speak on behalf of Martin Deane (Alliance), which will be my first intervention upon the hustings in my entire voting life. At least the fact that I shall be appearing with John Cleese and Barry Norman will help to establish that this is more of a variety show than a profound political forum.

But (now for something serious) I cannot abide the prospect of five more years of Mrs T. It's not just the scandal of 20% unemployment and the country being written off north of Leicester. To admit my deepest personal motives – which are what really count: 1) I have tried to interview Mrs T. and she simply does not listen to what one says. 2) She has squeezed out of the Conservative Party all of those – James Prior, Carrington, St John Stevas, Heath, etc. – who made it remotely tolerable. 3) She treats with contempt the institutes of culture, science and education which still give – or gave – this country some standing in the world. If she does win, I am afraid the worst effect of all will be that reasonable moderate men and women will have to leave politics altogether and we shall be reduced to a philistine, money-grabbing Right and a wrecking, reactionary Left. I'd like a parliament so hung up that the only way to run the country at all would be to leave almost everything alone (except for introducing proportional representation) and concentrate on making what we have already work properly. This ought to be called Conservatism. But what has the Conservative Party under Mrs T. actually conserved? Change and decay in all around I see.

May 20th–21st

The diary says I have two lectures to give in Lancaster, followed by one in Wakefield. So northward ho we go. I decide to give Lancaster University the definitive version of my spiel on The Importance of Saints, and the Methodists of Wakefield a rhapsody on Inner and Outer Peace which I'll rehearse on the Quakers of Lancaster the night before.

Much though I love my fellow Quakers – they really are *good* people – they do have this distressing tendency to be vegetarians and teetotallers and to take their latest meal at 6.30, which makes for a somewhat glum evening.

Retiring early to bed with a flask of whisky in the suitcase is scarcely more cheering, since instead of satisfaction all you get is disappointment followed by guilt.

But I am being disgustingly carnal. The chief thing that lured me to the North was the promise of a day's pilgrimage to the country between the original Pendle Hill in North Yorkshire and Swarthmore in Cumbria which George Fox, the founder of the Quakers, walked in the year 1652. I can assure any Quaker who has never seen that magic kingdom that the experience can bring 'verily great openings'.

It is not just that tracing the names and places which Fox mentions in his journal helps to convince you that yes, it really did happen as they say. Every religion owes something profound to the landscape of its origins, even to its native weather. Fox must have had unusually good weather that Whitsuntide, for it is not always that you get the far-ranging views that he got and which filled him with a sense of biblical revelation.

The journal tells us how George – his perceptions elevated by lack of food and drink – clambered up the steep side of Pendle Hill and was there moved 'to sound the Day of the Lord', as he did again upon Cader Idris five years later. Goodness knows what the sounding was like – there was no one else there to hear it – but what a sounding it must have been. High hills obviously intoxicated George, as well they might a visionary young man who had spent most of his life till then in the flat Midlands. All those psalmic references to the holy hills of God and their vistas of the Promised Land must have come flooding in upon him.

What Fox does not convey is the sinister vastness of Pendle Hill, with its long edge like an axe-head against the sky. Yet far from being oppressed by its evil reputation, he gained from it his first vision of 'a great people waiting to be gathered'. The sheer light within him overwhelmed the darkness of the spot, and showed him all the way to the sea (which he had never before viewed).

Then on he went circuitously to the hamlet of Briggflatts, where the flax growers fulfilled his dream of 'a people in white raiment by a river's side'; and then to the Whitsun hiring fair at Sedbergh, where his preaching drew comments that implied the Christly nature of his mission; and eventually to the site of the now vanished chapel on Firbank Fell, where upwards of a thousand Westmoreland Seekers – independent waiters-upon-God – had gathered. And there, speaking from the crag which still overlooks a natural amphitheatre on the hillside, Fox took his opportunity to become the teacher and leader of that movement-in-waiting. As at Sedbergh, he refused to go indoors and preach from the pulpit, telling them that even their simple chapel was unnecessary to God, whose only temple was their very selves. The Scriptures which had been imprisoned within the material church must be released, so that the free Spirit could blow through them once more and carry them into the wide world.

However much scholarship we recruit I doubt if we can ever fully share the Seekers' understanding. Our intellectual background is so different from theirs. But it is the Spirit, not the letter, that gives life. Standing upon that crag, with the clouds flying and shafts of light stabbing down into the surrounding valleys as if pointing out where God's people were, we cannot doubt that the very same Spirit which descended upon Fox and his hearers is there to bring light and life to us too. There is nothing over us, nothing between us and the Spirit, nothing except our reluctance to climb up there and invite it. Maybe we can't stand such reality for long. We have to climb down again like Fox and seek the sanctuary offered him by the kindly Judge Fell at Swarthmore Hall. But never to forget that 'I will lift up mine eyes unto the hills, from whence cometh my help . . .'

My puritan soul is greatly refreshed. This is where it belongs.

And then I drive on to Wakefield over the spacious Yorkshire landscape that southerners don't know exists. And I deliver my address about outer and inner peace in a deep, two-tier chapel like a synagogue. Standing there in the pulpit like the captain of a ship trying to talk the crew out of mutiny, I become aware that among the bewildered Methodists there are little pockets of purring Quakers. I suppose there are about 250 people in all, for northerners will still turn out to hear a public lecture during TV hours. Still, G. Fox, I'm afraid, would never have approved of such ministry within a steeple-house. I ought to be out there on the fells.

May 29th

From this morning's *Hampstead & Highgate Express* (which God preserve): 'Sergeant Brian Winterflood, the police officer who intended to push a 10ft-high inflatable canvas liver around the country for charity, has had to withdraw from his mammoth marathon after slipping a disc.' After that, he had no stomach for the task.

After lunch I motor down to Somerset, where I had carelessly promised (in the interests of ecumenism) to deliver a paper to a conference of Roman Catholics on 'Standards in the Media' – an old hobby-horse. The conference venue – at Ammerdown, near Wells – turns out as usual to resemble a prep school. It is staffed by nuns but is mercifully equipped with a bar. I don't mind taking my dirty plates back to the scullery and laying my own place for breakfast, but I'm damned if I'll make up the bed with clean sheets for the next occupant of my room. The centre has been adapted from the stables of a fairly stately home belonging to the Hiltons (whoever they are). One has access to the stately gardens with their maze of clipped hedges looking like the set for something by Michael Tippett. The first cuckoo I've heard for ages toots in the nearby woodlands. But it rains constantly.

There is a chapel adapted from what I take to have been a coach-house, more or less round, so that we sit in a ring looking inwards, which gives the familiar feeling of a Quaker meeting. But – oh dear! – in spite of a conscious effort to introduce more silence, Mass is still terribly chatty – especially as there are five priests present who will insist on 'concelebrating'. There's the usual 'cuddle of peace' in the middle of things, which I find embarrassing: even if one just shakes hands, saying 'Peace be with you, Friend', it's confusing for a Quaker because shaking hands is how we *end* the meeting. And the Catholic music! I suppose they missed out on the great hymn-writing periods of the seventeenth to nineteenth centuries, but I wish they would borrow from the protestant hymn-books instead of using the banal jingles they've cooked up recently, complete with guitar-strumming. People complain about trendiness in the C. of E. these days, but it's dignified compared with these do-it-yourself masses. However, they're good people, so I try to wrap myself in a private cocoon of quietness and shake hands when they're extended to me. Should I take the wafer? I'm pretty sure they'd give it to me, and I'd quite like to accept it as a sign of fraternity. However, that's not what it's meant to be in Catholic theology; and the gesture might get some priest into trouble with his bishop; so I stay in my private cocoon, trying to emanate benevolent vibrations.

There must be about forty there for the weekend: mostly women – some of them nuns engaged in church public relations, the rest regular conference groupies. The speakers are me (on broadcasting), Clive Thornton (on newspapers – he used to be chief executive of the *Mirror*), and Jim O'Connor (on advertising). The liveliest of the male participants is Kevin Grant, editor-in-chief of the Catholic *Universe*, with whom I hit it off well – to the extent of selling him a cut-down version of my address for his paper, so the effort of preparing it will not, thank goodness, have been unrewarding. There is also a gaunt Dominican philosopher, who lets nobody get away with nonsense. One morning I find him being greeted by the centre's black-and-white cat. 'It takes one to know one,' he says. The robes, you see. And there's a man with a distressing vocal tic, who makes encouraging little 'yoo- yoo- yoo-' noises in his throat all the time, even when you are not speaking to him. He is the second of this kind that I have met in a week – the first was a lady who went 'whee- whee- whee-'. I wonder how it would sound if they ever met.

Clive Thornton is a remarkable fellow, certainly if his own (unchallenged) account of his career is to be accepted. He does not have much to say about the morality of journalism as such, but a lot about the immorality or amorality of the various boards and managements he has been involved with, from the asset-stripping takeover men to the faceless pension funds who sell out to them. It seems that four wheeler-dealers own 80% of our newspapers, only one of whom is an English national with his company registered in Britain. The depressing conclusion is that big money always gets its way, and when a board swears it will never sell out to that stinker Mr Q., it will probably have done so by dawn the next day. The working journalist doesn't emerge from the Thornton story with any more honour – he's literally a hired hack. And as for the old Spanish customs of the printers – everything we have heard is true, and worse. But I had better not start quoting directly.

Compared with this, O'Connor made advertising sound positively virtuous and rigorously regulated. Did you know, for example, that you may not advertise claiming that certain exercises will make you taller? That you can't claim that the Queen actually *uses* any of the things bearing the royal warrant? That cigarette ads should not suggest any of the people in them are having sex together? That drink ads must never suggest that not drinking the stuff makes you a social outcast? That you mustn't claim copper bangles are good for rheumatism or that vitamins are any good applied to the skin? Legal, decent, honest and truthful it's all got to be. But that doesn't stop some of it being very, very ingenious.

My own bit harped on half-a-dozen favourite points:

1) That the influence of the media on society is grossly exaggerated. But people are determined to find their scapegoats.

2) We talk loftily about the media as communication, information, persuasion. But they are 90% entertainment.

3) The media may pose as a public service, but they are all *in business*.

4) The style of each medium is governed by its advantage and its limitations, especially those of its technology. Media people often become seduced by the mastering of technical skills to the neglect of what is being communicated.

5) Truth is easier said than found. The people who know it too often won't tell it. And the reporter seldom has time to go far enough back, deep enough down.

6) Blaming TV for violence doesn't hold water. You can't, anyway, separate out cause from effect in a continuum that stretches all the way back to Eden.

7) By and large, a nation gets the media it deserves. We are an ill-educated nation riddled with ignorance and bad taste, so it's a marvel the media are as good as they are. The market for quality papers and quality broadcasting *has* expanded with the expansion of university education since World War Two, but it's a slow and expensive business.

8) I'm all against letting reform of the media become a parliamentary hobby, with special media codes and media offences enforced by law. Use the off switch. Don't buy nasties. Keep nagging constructively at organisations like the BBC, but don't get hysterical about them.

49

9) I should be sorry if the media ever became entirely respectable. I think the press should always keep one foot in the gutter, because that's where the powerful throw their guilty secrets.

Oh – that's a bit more than half-a-dozen. I always put too much in my talks, and when I've finished there's a stunned silence and people ask could they have copies of the text to think about? When we break up into discussion groups, mine includes three ladies who recite a long list of television outrages – writhing bodies, obscene language, infidelity, treachery, cruelty . . . 'But how do you know about these things?' 'Oh – we watch them *all*.' One wonders why England isn't overrun with depraved middle-aged ladies, if what they say about the influence of TV is true.

After another guitar mass and prep-school lunch, I tip-toe away leaving my unmade bed. Perhaps the nuns will put me on their black list and not let me back.

June 2nd

The National Trust is giving a freebie. I'm invited to join a bus-load of travel and arts writers on a trip down to Knole to see James II's gold and silver bed which has been gloriously restored by two hundred volunteer ladies taking thirteen years. It really is a very good freebie (the Trust always does them well) and I comfort my conscience with the argument that us freelances need them more than the staff writers whose organisations could well afford to pay. A so-called 'executive coach' is waiting for us in Queen Anne's Gate and we roll off down the Old Kent road, eating smoked salmon sandwiches and drinking champagne, on our way to see a King's bed.

Knole is amazing. From a distance it resembles a fortified mediaeval town; closer to, a very large Oxford college. It started off as a palace for Archbishops of Canterbury; then Henry VIII fancied it. Elizabeth I gave it to the Sackvilles, who have been there ever since. One of them held some position at court which entitled him to any piece of furniture which was deemed to be worn, unworthy or out-of-date: hence Knole became stocked with appropriated royal bits and pieces, mostly Stuart, unmatched anywhere else. Including the bed, which must be the most beautiful bed in the world, hung with waterfalls of gold and crowned with fountains of ostrich-feather, not to mention its attendant mirrors, stools, dressing-tables and what not. The guide does not say who may have enjoyed the royal favours in it, but I guess it would have been worth almost any sacrifice to lie back in it, totally surrounded by gold, and think of the Bank of England.

Knole has quadrangle after quadrangle and at least three long galleries, hung with very inferior portraits of the kind used to illustrate children's history books. An exception is a powerful Reynolds of Samuel Johnson in middle age without a wig for a change. My favourite bit is the so-called Stone Court which has leaden rainwater pipes dated 1608 – beautifully detailed, and each one fitted with a little sliding hatch just below a bend, so that you can unblock it of dead leaves. Admittedly the interior is rather dark and chilly – I think they keep it that way to help preserve the fabrics. One reason for the remarkable preservation of the contents is that whenever the Sackvilles got bored with any of it, they just pulled the dust-sheets over it and moved on to another wing. Hence the story that not so long ago relatives coming to stay were put up at the local inn on the grounds that there wasn't a room to spare out of the 365 in Knole.

The quadrangles are full of middle-aged ladies who had been recruited locally to come and pick the royal bedhangings apart, clean them, re-back them, re-work the embroidery and reassemble it all. They are justly proud of their handiwork which has turned Knole, it is said, into the world's top fabric conservatory. They show us their workshop, the size of a small factory, hidden away under the rafters of yet another quadrangle, but gleaming with up-to-date equipment. 'We are hoping', says one of them, 'to get our teeth into the Venetian Ambassador's bed next . . .'

There's tea and cakes, followed by speeches and toastings (more champagne), and the cutting of an iced cake made in the image of the said bed. I potter off to the National Trust gifte shoppe in the Henry VIII courtyard and buy some genuine Knole pot-pourri, which I guess they needed to overpower the pong of insanitary Sackvilles. Tipped into a bowl back at home it is remarkably influential.

Apart from the rain it is a very agreeable outing. Sue Arnold uses it at length for her column the following Sunday, including the champagne and smoked salmon in the Old Kent Road.

June 4th

Sylvia feels the urge to go down to Cornwall and visit Diana, whose baby is due in about a month's time. So I'm on my own for three days. On the Thursday night I lose my political virginity in Bath. Malcolm Dean – a *Guardian* journalist – is standing there for the Alliance and has asked me, John Cleese and Barry Norman to do a little cabaret for him as 'Stars for Dean'. We are to perform in a disused railway station, which sounds depressing but turns out to be rather good. At least, it is for me, though I don't know how Cleese found it since he never arrives while I am there. All we hear of him is agonised telephone calls from traffic jams on the M4.

Barry Norman (a very nice man with a very nice wife to match) introduces me as the man who knows which side God's on. Well, I tell them under the Representation of the People Act, God – like peers, bankrupts and lunatics – hasn't got a vote. But I've called the Heavenly press office (they put me on hold and fed me a burst of the Hallelujah Chorus while I waited) and an official spokesangel has assured me that the Heavenly Host is solidly behind the Alliance. Wild cheers from my audience. Yes, I say, a random sample of saints and martyrs has revealed 82% Alliance (including, of course, all the four St Davids), 11% Tory (real reactionaries like St Paul and St Augustine of Hippo), and 7% Labour (headed by St Francis of Assisi, on account of the Labour promise to abolish blood sports). Were the Cherubim and Seraphim pro-Alliance? 'Wholly, wholly, wholly . . .' they said. Then a slightly rude bit about being allergic to Mrs Thatcher because she reminded me of the matron who used to come round my prep school every morning asking the little boys if they had opened their bowels and prescribing syrup of figs if they hadn't. Ending with a slightly pompous bit about how dare the Tories call themselves conservatives – for what had they actually conserved? Not hospitals, schools, universities, the arts, law and order. They claimed to have spent all this money on us, but where had it gone? They didn't even seem to be a very efficient government. Moral: Be on the side of the angels – for Heaven's sake, vote Alliance!

I think only the converted were there anyway, but they loved it. Dean is said to have quite a good chance in Bath and says his meetings and debates have been well-attended. Whatever may be happening elsewhere, the election in Bath isn't confined to TV. I think this may have something to do with the feeling of the place as a city state.

Watching the television till after midnight each night, you can't deny that the networks are busting themselves to 'debate the issues' responsibly and educate the electorate. But the party managers, whatever they may say about the primacy of policy, seem determined to run the campaign as a beauty contest – look now upon this picture and on this . . . Kinnock sparkles away (still more does the pretty Mrs K.), but Mrs. T. seems cross at having to explain herself at all instead of being bowed back into Downing Street as a matter of right. She keeps talking about having *two* more terms, but she seems to have aged considerably over the past months, and although she never was much good at hearing what other people say to her, I wonder if she isn't actually going deaf?

June 7th

I visit a dear friend who is suffering from depression, who sits there doped up to the eyebrows, senses muffled, wit worn out. It is unspeakably sad but there *is* light at the end of the tunnel if only the doctors can hit on the right approach, which might be anything from drugs to diet or biding one's time to unburdening oneself on the couch. If you ask me, psychiatry is barely in its teens.

Sylvia comes back from Cornwall having kitted out Diana for the baby. D. seems fine, she reports, though getting rather bored with the final weeks. I'm glad she has decided to retire permanently from shoving those enormous cows around. Instead, she has her personal collection of calves now installed on some land rented from Camborne Council – plus the two horses, six ducks, two dogs and one cat. Diana has told Sylvia she fancies four children, but it is not clear whether Raymond has yet been told. D. is a natural nest-maker and brooder. I think Raymond's great appeal for her is his reliability. Nothing flashy or romantic, though they have much fun together. Certainly not much money, but they live simply, eat heartily and manage ingeniously in the country manner of swapping favours. Top of any father's demands for his daughter should come (as I see now) devotion and dependability.

June 8th

The whites of duck-eggs make brilliant meringue. The yolks make brilliant *crème brulée*. Two ways of killing yourself with the same egg.

In three days' time I am supposed to be leaving for Caracas, Venezuela, with Ros and Martin of CTVC, to film some more homelessness. I ring up Ros and detect nasty signs of history repeating itself. Like the Indians, the Venezuelans are feeling twitchy about us: possibly, it is thought, the risk of our being there during some sort of political disorder. It's understandable that some governments fear that cameras from more stable countries may hold them up to ridicule and contempt. We would all like to sweep our disasters under the carpet. But in fact these governments would get a much better press if they stopped worrying about the press they got.

So long as there is still a chance we may be going on Thursday I must stock up the suitcase with enough reading material this time. I almost went mad in Lusaka for lack of it.

June 9th

Our poll cards arrive. As usual we vote at the Tea House in the middle of Hampstead Garden Suburb. This has not actually served teas for many years, though it originally did under the distinguished management of a firm called Messrs Bikkiepegs Ltd to whom the contract was awarded by our founder, Dame Henrietta Barnett. The Dame was a firm believer in temperance and the Tea House was the closest thing she would allow to having a pub in her paradise. But it expired, so now we have neither tea nor beer – nor indeed a decent pub within a mile of us. The Tea House is used as a kind of village hall.

No question but that we'll vote Alliance. 'Win with Monroe Palmer' says the orange poster on the front of our house. But I doubt that we will. There is a strong Gaitskellite streak among the Anglo-Saxons round here and the Labour Left frightens them; but the Jewish and Hindu vote must be solidly Tory. Mrs T. is just up the road in Finchley, surrounded by the biggest Jewish community in Britain, and knows which side her bread is kosher buttered. I have been ambushed twice by the Tory candidate, a stockbroking MEP called John Marshall, outside the Waitrose supermarket. 'I hope you'll be voting for me on the eleventh?' 'I very much doubt it,' I said; hastily adding, 'but I wish you well.'

'But you don't, do you?' asked Sylvia, later, incapable as always of telling a lie. 'I just couldn't be rude to the man,' I said, 'it must be an awful life being an MP.' And when I did my Thought for the Day on Radio 4, I invited the listeners to say a little prayer for the wretched politicians we've been kicking around for the past month, at least two-thirds of whom will shortly have their hearts broken.

June 11th

Roll up that map of Venezuela – I shall not be needing it before September, if then. What with Jennet's cancer treatment and Diana's baby, not going does have certain advantages. But it's dislocating, leaves idle holes in the diary, and has friends staring at me in disbelief saying, 'But I thought you were in . . .'

At least I can vote at leisure, making my mark for Monroe and patting the ballot paper into the black box in the Tea House. The Alliance clearly hasn't a hope even of holding the balance. For anything like that to happen both the other parties would have had to discredit themselves – and they haven't. they've devoted great attention to not making mistakes. Personally I think it would have been better if the social Democrats had accepted baptism as Liberals long ago; but I suppose it was too soon for the defectors from the Labour Party to admit that their snowball never snowballed and has been melting steadily ever since. Poor dear Shirley adds yet another to her list of losses. Roy Jenkins can stop pretending he belongs to Glasgow. And whoever was Bill Rodgers, anyway? Only David Owen survives, gleaming like a well-honed hatchet.

Labour and Tory have campaigned cunningly. Labour managed to keep its 'loonies' gagged and bound so far as the national stage was concerned (though we'll be hearing a lot more of them in due course, I think). The party ran Neil for President, invariably with the vivacious Glenys by his side. The Tories must have spent millions just making themselves look the Party in Power, and carefully did not wheel out the Boss too often. But when all is said and done, it's the *embourgeoisement* of Britain that's decisive.

I stay up till four in the morning in front of the television, and you can see it on the map. Middle-classification is eating its way up the country from the south coast. Its front line has got as far as Wolverhampton, and there are already pockets north of that. The Labour Party will never get back to power again as a working-class bloc, because the working-class is moving fast up-market and breaking up as it goes. There may be three million unemployed, but there are vastly more who are at work and earning well; and the unemployed are remarkably docile. In spite of complaints about the schools and the health service (where *did* all that money go that the government says it spent on them?), I think there's a collective guilty conscience about the extravagant days of 'full employment' and trade union debauchery that prevents people stampeding to Labour. Very many people are still allergic to the unions and likely to remain so for some time to come. Certain of them – the teachers, civil servants and Screaming Lord Scargill – show signs of getting uppity once more, and I can see a re-elected

Mrs T. pushing them to the breaking point if they're unwise enough to invite it.

June 12th

I get to bed as dawn is oozing through the grey skies. David Dimbleby and Co. are still as high as kites on their strings of statistics (which, incidentally, they got badly wrong in the early stages). Mrs T. will have a majority of 102 over everyone else, which will do nicely, thank you, though it must be troublesome getting wiped out in Scotland. On the other hand I don't envy Mr K. for the bunch he's got stuck with. What *is* the Labour Party going to *do* for the next four or five years? Draft a neo-Marxist constitution for Scotland? Still, the future is quite inscrutable. In a couple of years' time the government may be on its knees for reasons yet undreamed of.

After lunch I visit Jennet who is having drugs dripped into her at the Royal Free. She is pathetically brave and even contrives a little comedy; but it is too much like witnessing a crucifixion. *Stabat pater dolorosus . . .* Her treatment does not end till nearly midnight when, stupefied and vomiting, the hospital sends her home to her flat because, you see, there is no bed free in the cancer ward.

June 13–20th

A week of hack-work, bits and pieces, and more or less continuous rain. Jennet and her faithful Ed – for whom I have a growing regard, he's helping her carry a heavy load – take off for a week down at Carfury where I have no doubt it is raining even harder.

June 21st

A taxi collects me at half-past-six for the *Sunday* programme, anchored by Jill Cochran and Ted Harrison. Ted has one of the sharpest *quiet* minds in the business; no one would guess that he's kept alive by dialysis and desperately needs a new kidney. Jill, I'm proud to say, I helped to discover some years ago when she sent in a taped talk on being a Jewish mother married to a Catholic. I don't do much to help my fellow humans, but that was one of my better efforts.

I chatter through a review of the week's religious press – each denomination counting up its adherents in the new parliament. Lots of Catholics, Methodists and Jews. Only one Baptist. The Established Church makes no claim at all, presumably on the grounds that everyone else automatically counts as C. of E. I give my prize for the week's comic story to the Quakers, who have just issued a booklet on ways of fostering non-violence in society. It contains a splendid tip on what to do when you're walking along a dark street and hear a would-be mugger coming up behind: you whip the lid off the nearest dustbin and conduct a conversation with an imaginary person inside. This so disconcerts the mugger that he shuffles off muttering. Alternatively, I suppose, you could do a little dance or recite 'The Wreck of the Hesperus' in a strong Australian accent. Try it some time.

In the course of the programme I am asked to comment on the annual druidic capers at Stonehenge and am moved to say that I find them totally silly – as silly as freemasonry, which is currently being taken far too seriously by the Church of England in a report which deems the masons to be blasphemous and heretical. *I* think they are childish and ridiculous, and so are the druids and latter-day solstice freaks, though the Church has itself to blame if people prefer such fictitious cults to its own mythology. British masonry (the continental varieties are another, more sinister matter) is a shallow theism that grew out of the Age of Reason. Druidry has even shallower roots, a nineteenth-century concoction which can have no real connection with the original druids for the simple reason that they couldn't write and we have no idea *what* they believed. Caesar says they used to burn people in wickerwork idols, which was nasty rather than silly. Anyhow, I dwell on the silliness of our own dear druids (and masons) and in due course get several letters saying that Quakers ought to be more tolerant – signed by Quakers. I am afraid there is a tendency among Friends to put up with nonsense in the name of broad-mindedness. Well, I tolerate it – the world is full of rubbish that one has no option but to tolerate – but I'm damned if I'll pretend to agree with it when someone asks me.

June 23rd

To the opera with Sylvia and George and Irene Engle, to see Shostakovitch's *Lady Macbeth of Mtsensk* – the one that offended Stalin and was banned for thirty years. I think Stalin was upset by the realism of the prison camp in the last act; that it wasn't anything to do with the alleged muddle of musical styles.

Yet again, I'm afraid, the opera is grossly disfigured by one of the ENO's demon producers. We have already had *Rusalka* set in Freud's nursery and the *Magic Flute* in the Codrington Library: now, instead of a mid-nineteenth-century merchant's warehouse we get a chromium-plated meat-packing plant with the chorus sawing up carcases and, for kicks, sodomising dead pigs. As an unnecessary gesture to the Macbeth in the title, three non-singing witches are introduced. What the hell they are doing in a slaughterhouse is far from clear.

Still, I'm glad to have heard the music which was impressive without being memorable. Shostakovitch must have had a prodigal budget to work with, because from time to time a platoon of extra brass marches on stage and blasts all before it. George (his wit fully recovered from a recent spell in the dumps) remarks, 'Someone must have told him where there's muck there's brass.'

June 25th

Another dash down to Cornwall where I had promised to 'open' the annual fete in aid of the Penzance subscription library (founded 1818 and still tottering on). Needless to say it rains persistently, so I have to make my little speech half-way up the staircase instead of out in the garden. As one gets older, I say, one is increasingly struck by the absurdities of life. I tell them about the absurd telephone at the British High Commission in Lusaka; about the absurd experience of sitting on the lavatory 30,000 feet up in an airliner; about the total absurdity of television which has cost billions of pounds worth of human ingenuity to develop and which, when you turn it on, shows you the red-headed Duchess of York jumping up and down or a commercial for safe sex. Everyone *knows* the secret of safe sex (I remind them) – you stop the car first. That's why they have things called lay-bys. A guffaw from Lord St Levan who has left Lady St Levan back on St Michael's Mount preparing supper for 150 tenants.

Jennet and Ed have refreshed themselves up at Carfury and return to London. Sylvia checks anxiously on Diana whose baby could be any day now. Apart from feeling rather bored she is in fine shape – well, actually her *shape* is very far from *fine*, but let's say in good health. She takes us for a walk from her cottage outside Camborne to inspect her collection of calves and heifers. One of them, a soulful Jersey called Amy, is also pregnant. Diana leads the way over fences and gates until we come to a green valley beside the Camborne by-pass where the little herd is safely grazing as the cars whizz over their heads. 'We managed to rent it cheap from the Council because there's a cess-pit in the middle. Still, it's a beginning,' says Diana with dreams of acres yet to come.

June 29th

Back from Cornwall to find some useful cheques in the post that should make the bank manager happier. First little job at the typewriter is to compose an introduction to a book that Patrick Forbes – my researcher on *Priestland's Progress* – has written about Holy Clowning. Apparently, there is quite a movement, on both sides of the Atlantic, of clergymen who believe the best way to spread the gospel is to put on baggy trousers and a red nose and make a fool of yourself. Personally I'm not too keen on clowns, having been scared stiff by one at Bertram Mills Circus when I was four: they seem to me part demonic, part undignified, part plain silly. But the holy fools have stretched their theology so far that there are certainly bits of it I can go along with. I'm all for jokes in church, for going over the top occasionally, for not being afraid of saying things about God that sound disrespectful to the stuffy. Anyway, besides being a lunatic on the surface, Patrick is actually a wise and wily priest.

July 1st

The telephone goes at 8.15 am. I know immediately what it must be. *Nobody* rings at 8.15 am. And sure enough it is Raymond – incoherently Cornish – announcing that Diana gave birth to an eight-pound daughter at twenty past five this morning.

Sylvia and I start dashing around like ants in a disturbed ants-nest. Appointments are cancelled, neighbours recruited to feed cats; within three hours we are in the train for Truro and its hospital at Treliske. Twelve hours after the birth of our first grandchild, we are crouched over the crib, drooling. She is quite perfect (not one of those grotesque changelings) with red hair, her grandfather's long hands and feet, and a neat little clarinet-player's mouth. When she cries, she doesn't work herself up to it but silently changes colour, then opens her mouth and lets rip. A little rocking usually stops it.

Diana herself looks well but feels tired. It wasn't easy – I won't go into gruesome details, but Raymond was in attendance after the modern manner and by all accounts was the required pillar of strength. Which makes me guiltily aware that I never was – in fact was usually several thousand miles away when needed.

Grandfathers – if not fathers – are best in the background at times like these, whence I observe a new kind of look between Diana and Sylvia that says, 'Well, now we both know it all, don't we?' But this grandfather still claims the right to his private rhapsody. For suddenly our sixties are transformed: it's no longer downhill all the way to the cemetery, but upwards into the spring sunlight. Welcome, little one, to the huge fun of life. Start living and enjoying it today. Don't let them tell you that childhood is just a preparation for the real thing: it's as real now as you'll ever know. Believe me, in spite of the upheaval you've just been through, it's more fun out of the womb than in it. Up to now your existence has been cosy and carefree, but frankly rather dull. You ain't *seen* nothing yet, nor smelt, nor felt, nor tasted nor heard much more than a mumble. Now, for a start, there are delicious breasts to nuzzle (make the most of them and they'll stand you in good stead, one way and another, all your life). Later there will be pussy-cats to stroke and flowers to sniff, water to splash in, stories to hear, music to dance to and, later still, books to read and music to play for yourself. Best of all, there will be other people to love – and you don't get *that* in the womb.

P.S. I may not be there to see it myself, but your mother already wants you to be a vet.

After some debate, Raymond and Diana decide to call her Jennet Natasha Priestland-Hearn, and she is thus solemnly announced in *The Times* – to the confusion, no doubt, of my *Telegraph*-reading relatives.

July 2nd–3rd

We visit Diana once or twice a day, feeling a little self-conscious among the standard-sized-shaped-voiced Cornish mums and their visitors: but then Diana herself is way off standard. It's too far to Carfury and we haven't a car, so Sylvia and I stay at what appears to be the only hotel in Truro, which is a useful city but not a lot of fun. At five o' clock every evening it becomes instant Sunday. Even the ducks on the river go home, and we are reduced to spinning out our over-rich dinners and watching television in bed.

The train back to London on the Friday evening is two hours late. A jolly steward in the restaurant car deserves a bonus for keeping us happy, producing miraculous extras like Welsh rarebit and cream for the coffee. On the whole I enjoy rumbling through the West Country, eating as I go and inspecting the crops, but after dark it may as well be Siberia.

Must get baby-snaps quickly developed, so I can become a fully-equipped kiddy-bore.

July 4th

After the wettest June on record it has stopped raining. An explosion of roses. A resurrection of geraniums. Mosel-and-soda under the apple trees in the garden. I feel so invigorated that I decide to spend some money on myself, which I don't do very often. For years now I have been wearing a very cheap, very plain, very reliable Japanese wrist-watch which has never let me down but suddenly strikes me as being typical of a sixth-form swot. I shall blossom forth with something glamorously new. So into the jeweller's on Finchley Road – hurrah! a sale! – and out again wearing a slightly less cheap, less plain, but (I am assured) equally reliable Japanese watch in pseudo-gold. At once I feel vulgar, extravagant, awful.

Further alarm is created by a telephone call from my bank. Had I not received their invitation to a party, on the premises, next Tuesday? A *what*? A party. Yes, *in* the bank. Wine, soft drinks, light snacks, as the guest of (yours very sincerely) the Manager. Could I come? Feeling rather like a delinquent prefect summoned to dine with the headmaster, what can I do but accept?

July 7th

It's true, there really *is* a party at my bank, though I hardly dare believe it. I approach the place sceptically at six on the dot, and it looks as uptight as ever. But then two men in suits walk up and ring the bell, and the doors swing open and, behold! Revelry! There's old Mr Dennis with a glass in his hand as greeter, and behind him the Manager with an even bigger glass. It's like something from the Prohibition era. The canapés are terrific – cascades of them all over the Manager's desk – and back in that sinister corner where they go to ask the computer whether it trusts you, there are rows and rows of glasses with beaded bubbles winking at the brim.

The bank wasn't originally designed to double as a pub, though, and what with the bandit-proof screens and heavy security doors it is a little difficult to circulate freely. The girl clerks passing round the canapés brush their breasts deliciously across one's belly as they squeeze by. The other guests seem to be either local shopkeepers or men from the bank's head office, come to spy on customer relations. I'm not sure why I was invited, being heavily in the red. Indeed, the assistant manager introduces me to some area boss as the '*notorious* Gerald Priestland', though whether for theological or financial reasons isn't clear. Anyhow, I break nervously into my song-and-dance routine and offer to make them a TV commercial on the slogan 'Natwest – the bank that likes to say Cheers!' or maybe 'The bank that makes you drunk'.

It all smells like a plot to make us love our bank, which I think is unnatural. It doesn't fool young Mr Cohen who sold me my watch the other day and is here as part of the party. 'Why don't the banks put up the fifty-pound limit on cheque cards?' he demands. 'I'll tell you why not – they want to force people into using their Access cards on which the bank will collect at least three per cent.' The bank man we are talking to sheepishly nods his head. All the same, it's an unexpectedly good party and after more than enough jokes about liquid assets and, 'I take it you're deep in the red, old boy?' I roll home, thankful it's near enough for me not to have to drive.

July 9th

There are so many flowers out now, the garden looks quite vulgar. Mr Hiskey, the visiting gardener, announces with disbelief that it hasn't rained for eighteen days.

July 12th

I am to make an appearance on Henry Kelly's breakfast TV show, from TV-am down at Chalk Farm. A weird building – a sort of high tech warehouse loosely filled with nursery equipment and potted trees. The actual television goes on in one corner.

The indomitably cheerful Henry I've known since he worked with me on the old Newsdesk programme in BBC Radio. My fellow guest is that cuddly comrade, Ken Livingstone. We are supposed to discuss secrecy in government, me as an expert on the United States Congress and 'Irangate', Ken as the MP who dared to suggest the British government was trying to hush up some dirty tricks in Northern Ireland. We manage to fill the time quite agreeably, but as Henry says afterwards, 'You can only make *one* very simple point in a TV interview, and you've got to make it three times.'

Ken is a charming snake. For all his outrage over counter-subversion, you can be quite sure that, come the revolution, Ken and his friends will immediately create a Bureau of Public Security to protect the People from their class enemies. He professes to be unimpressed by parliament. 'The moment I walked in there, the Tories were all over me, shaking me by the hand – till I realised they all wanted me for a pair. They don't seem to realise Labour members don't spend every other evening at a dinner party. Actually I seem to be far more hated on my own side of the House. It's all the media exposure I get. Colleagues say, "Why don't *I* get invited on the box?", and I tell them, "It's because you're so bloody boring".'

We ponder the question of why Bryan Gould is being so widely praised for the way he ran Labour's election campaign. After all, they *lost*. We agree that in fact people judged it as pure television – they didn't care for the product but loved the commercials.

Ken, it transpires, is allergic to monosodium glutamate.

July 13th

I desert my typewriter for a couple of hours picking soft fruit for the freezer. There's a farm beside the A41, just outside King's Langley, where we go every year (if we remember) and come back with enough currants, rasp-berries and gooseberries to last the winter. There are strawberries too, but these don't freeze so well – they go soggy when you thaw them, whereas the raspberries look marvellously fresh.

Picking makes a pleasant change from typing; and that particular countryside, where I was brought up, is full of nostalgia. Nicholas Brakespeare, the only English pope, was born there, too. I shall be back again – at Berkhamsted, a few miles up the road – to read *Pilgrim's Progress* at the memorial service for my cousin Frank Cooper, on Thursday. No funeral is complete without me these days.

July 14th

Our current tele-viewing rift: Sylvia wants to watch the report of Jeffrey Archer and the prostitute – I want to watch Colonel Ollie North versus the United States Constitution. By channel-hopping we usually manage to get both, the low comedy as well as the courtroom drama. I particularly liked the exchange: 'Are you quite sure you recognise Mr Archer?' 'Well, I spent ten minutes on top of him, so I should.' Then there was the judge who quite understood clients wanting the lady to dress up as a *nurse*, but not as a *matron*.

The North business is simply hair-raising, not least because so many Americans seem to think he's a hero and ought to run for president. I suppose the Marine Corps epitomises the machismic philosophy of 'Get in there and *win*' on which American fathers bring up their sons; and the US public must find it deeply satisfying that Rambo is alive and living in Washington. But it really *isn't* constitutional to circumvent the will of the Congress or try to set up an ultra-CIA by private subscription. I hope Congress has the guts not to be frightened off its duty by popular chauvinism.

July 16th

St Peter's, Berkhamsted, for the memorial service to Frank Cooper – my cousin, though he was nearly old enough to have been my father. He was a nice guy; a chemist by training who led the scientific side of the family sheep-dip business. When it was bought up by the Wellcome Foundation, Frank and his wife Dorothy settled in Provence and I scarcely saw them for twenty years. There is a baronetcy (not the most distinguished of titles) in the family on account of services rendered to the Conservative party, and I think Frank was 'the third baronet'. His son Richard – *Sir* Richard, indeed – seems to have assumed the title effortlessly and is suavely ushering relatives into the church as we arrive. Berkhamsted is not a bad little place. I used to feel furtive when I visited it, remembering childhood follies committed there, but now I'm at peace with it.

St Peter's looks quite imposing – all knapped flint on the outside and big enough inside for at least a suffragan to instal his throne. There are a couple of good brasses, one to Sir John Raven, squire to the Black Prince who held the castle at Berkhamsted. But the mediaeval paintings that must once have crowded the walls have all gone; it should not look so plain.

Goodness knows how many Cooper/Priestland family weddings and funerals I have attended here; even a christening or two, including my own. They've got a new organ, I see, and brought the altar forward to under the crossing. But who *are* all these people? Not only relatives but old

Cooper employees and retainers, cooks, nannies, chauffeurs (there used to be one called Partridge who drove the Rolls). I'm in despair at the thought of having to introduce them to Sylvia afterwards. *She* has six brothers and sisters whom we see quite often, but not much else. I have neither brother nor sister, but sheaves of cousins and sub-cousins whom I hardly ever see and can never put names to. When I do get a handle on one, he or she goes and dies.

I go up to the brass eagle and do my reading from *The Pilgrim's Progress*. Not all the trumpets sounding on the other side, which I did for Frank's brother Bill (the second baronet), but a passage that has always appealed to me much more, describing the departure of Mr Ready-to-Halt, a modest character who has nothing to leave but his crutches and whose parting words are 'Welcome life!'. Halfway through the reading my eyes catch those of Dorothy, sitting in the front pew, and I can see that *she* knows that *I* know that *she* knows that I am trying to squeeze all I can out of it, just short of making her cry. She is a very bright lady indeed – she was certainly the making of Frank – and we quite enjoy our little conspiracy.

Afterwards, up the hill to the old Cooper family mansion on the edge of Berkhamsted Common, which Wellcome have turned into a rather aristocratic research station for agricultural pharmacy. A flock of beautifully laundered sheep with long woolly tails is browsing in the paddock and even the old water-garden is carefully maintained. We mill about on the terrace with glasses of white wine and platters of salad, uttering little cries of feigned recognition and telling each other we really must meet again before the next funeral. Fortunately most people remember my late father who was regarded as the family eccentric, largely on the grounds of having publicly joined the Labour Party. He took a delight in shocking the Coopers' upper-class pretensions and once persuaded the village bus to drive him, in full evening dress, up to the front door for a dinner party.

Cunningly I get each cousin I meet to identify some other figure in the distance for me: 'Tell me, Barbara, who is that young man in the blue-grey suit? Mark? Ah, Mark! Good to see you again. Tell me, who is that stunning blonde in the white dress? Not Daphne! Why, Daphne . . .' And so I weave my detective trail through the forgotten tribe. But I have a hard time on the way back to London, trying to answer Sylvia's 'But exactly where does Daphne fit in?' questions.

July 17th

We break our journey down to Cornwall in Bristol, where our son Oliver is launching himself as an impresario ('Our Son the Impresario' we hope to be saying, as we cannot, for the moment, describe him as much else in particular). Oliver, while having no pretensions to act himself, is fascinated by theatrical production and believes he has identified a gap in Bristol's cultural market: there is no night-life. So he is hiring the basement of a disco called Harper's Bazaar, where he is putting on a four-act cabaret consisting of a band, a local comedy duo called Wack and Zane (popular on the Bristol after-dinner circuit), a feminist comedienne, and the Brown Paper Bag Brothers. But will anyone come?

Indeed, ought parents to be there at all? Will their ancient grey faces turn crimson with embarrassment? Sylvia and I cringe with anticipation, expecting something in the nature of north country club comedy. But Oliver assures us No – this is *alternative* humour from which all sexism, racism and excretism has been purged. And so – by and large – it turns out. The feminist comedienne feels obliged to say 'penis' three times and 'fucking' rather more, to show how liberated she is, but the rest is positively gentle. Some of the alternatives to humour would never have struck me as humorous before and still don't, however they rock the rest of the audience. Wack and Zane are deliberately incompetent jugglers, while the Brown Paper Bag Brothers extract a great deal of harmless fun from – brown paper bags. Interestingly, political satire seems of no interest to any of the artistes. Oliver complains there is not enough heckling from the audience.

Anyway, the ambiance is convincingly night-clubby: lots of little tables, spotlights, mirrors, entertainers moving amongst the patrons. A great deal of hard work has been put into publicity, and to Oliver's delight his thesis is proved: some 350 young professional Bristolians stump up their three-pound-fifty to get in, and on the second night it's a total sell-out and the bouncers are turning people away. It all goes so well that the management of the disco say that in future they'll be satisfied with the bar profits and Oliver can put his shows on there without further fee. This first experiment only runs two nights, but it clears a handsome profit and Our Son the Impresario is planning another bill for September featuring (among other turns) a Marxist magician.

We can't actually stay the night with Oliver and his girlfriend Natasha, because they have the Brown Paper Bags in their flat. Instead we secure bed and breakfast chez Mrs Scroggins whose period bathroom contains a prim notice requesting 'Please leave the bath as you would wish to find it.' At bargain price Mrs S. sends us on our way lined with the sort of traditional bacon-egg-and-sausage breakfast one is forbidden at home.

July 18th

Arrived in West Cornwall, the next few days are largely devoted to intensive baby-worship, Diana now being back home with the baby Jennet, an infant who prefers to keep her eyes shut and her mouth wide open – either for the emission of demands for the bottle or for the admission of the bottle demanded. As previously stated she is, nevertheless, the best-looking and most talented baby west of the Tamar, the Severn, the Thames. I will also record (and this should be worth checking later in her career) that in the interests of social adaptability she is being brought up on the principle of 'Who wants a go with the baby?' Whoever happens to be around gets her thrust into his or her arms with instructions to put down the last couple of ounces or bring up a burp or two. Her father, Raymond, is as Cornish and horny-handed as any character from Quiller-Couch, but I have seen no yuppie daddy in London more skilled at feeding and nappy-changing. And along comes Oliver – literally flushed with success from Harper's Bazaar – and handles his niece with all the finesse of a paediatrician. It is all very charming and I hope it continues like this long after Sylvia and I have moved on. The Family is much fawned upon these days (in theory), but in my view it's hardly a family at all if it amounts to no more than a mother, a father and one or two children. The family is a sprawling conglomerate of parents, grandparents, uncles, aunts, cousins and honorary hangers-on, who don't have to explain or be explained but share the communal burdens and pleasures as a matter of course. I hope it does work out that way for little Jennet.

July 22nd

We spend a good deal of time in Cornwall simply existing: chopping down weeds so as to get the car in and out, so as to drive down to Penzance, so as to order gas cylinders and food, so as to cook meals, so as to have the strength to chop down more weeds.

Time has to be spent, too, simply touching base with various friends and acquaintances. Over to St Just, where we meet Allan Holden, a retired BBC colleague with whom

I was engaged in a scheme to start a community radio station in Penzance – until horrid Mr Tebbit and his friends, having led us up the garden path, pushed us into the manure heap and called the whole thing off. Allan takes us to his favourite pub where we are introduced to an evil-looking bull terrier which had to leave town in a hurry having bitten a Pakistani in Penzance. Or that is what Allan says, though the landlord cries that the case was 'not proven'. The dog wags his tail enthusiastically at the memory of it. Allan then fills us in on the absorbing story of a recent Cornish vicar, who also left town, leaving behind a wife and several children. A bishop once told me that kind of thing was the worst part of his job. Doubts about the Trinity were a pushover in comparison.

After that we went to call on a really contented man – Scott Marshall, who makes pottery down at Boscean, half a mile outside St Just. Handsome, usable stuff it is and he's quite content to sit at his wheel turning out perfect copy after perfect copy and selling it to whoever turns up. You would think he'd have to ship it off to some big store in London to make ends meet, but he hates tearing himself away to do the marketing, and he would rather sell at what he regards as a fair price (actually it's absurdly cheap) than see the store's mark-up on it. Whenever he opens a kiln, word goes round the neighbourhood. If you, reader, get wind of it Boscean is well worth tracking down.

July 23rd

We lunch at Carbis Bay, where the beach is crowded with bodies flattened behind coloured windbreakers, then descend upon St Ives. At the Penwith Gallery – the local *avant-garde* art market – we find Roy Walker, two of whose prints we bought four years ago, and to cut a long afternoon short we end up in his studio overlooking Porth Meor, buying yet another. Roy, I think, would be much better known than he is but for two reasons: like Scott Marshall he can't be bothered to take time off from working in order to tramp round the London studios and market his stuff; and he develops so rapidly that he's never settled down to producing a recognisable Roy Walker line that people can accept as being 'in fashion'. And he, too – not that I'm complaining – is ludicrously cheap. The print we bought would have been more than reasonable at twice the price. But it is done in a technique which makes it impossible to reproduce – it is number one in an edition of one – so that if it's as good as Sylvia and I consider it to be, it should have cost at least five times what we paid. Thank heaven for artists like Roy and Scott. I only hope they can keep on paying the rent.

July 25th

Because it seems churlish to keep saying No, I said Yes to an invitation to preach at the annual service of the Cornwall Council of Churches in Gwennap Pit. The Pit is an extraordinary amphitheatre outside Redruth – a completely circular terraced crater in the open air, seating up to a thousand people, where John Wesley preached more than a dozen times and which has consequently become a Cornish holy place (though I bet it was also used for cock-fighting).

I feel ill at ease as an evangelist – my weaknesses are all too obvious to any who know me well – but it is rewarding to have a visible audience for a change. Broadcasting is like bowling without a batsman. Besides, I guess I ought to expose myself to a live public from time to time, if only to get the feel of whether anyone is really listening, let alone understanding what I'm trying to say.

We fumble our way through the lanes above Redruth, bump through a farmyard, and to our amazement find ourselves in a crowd of some five hundred people jostling towards the Pit. Learnedly, I explain to Sylvia that it must have been constructed in the middle ages for the Cornish Mystery Plays. But apparently not. They say it's the result of mine subsidence, which is mildly alarming.

I had hoped to find a brass band accompanying some good old Methodist hymns. But – *O tempora, O mores!* – we have the hymns without the brass, the accompaniment being provided by a rock-and-roll drum set and a trio of electric guitars led by a dog-collared priest. 'Thou whose almighty word Chaos and darkness heard' turns into a lilting waltz, while 'Lord, thy word abideth' is utterly destroyed by the band's attempts to drive it into a rock beat. I had requested these hymns as the build-up to my (reconditioned) sermon on 'The Word of God and the words of Man' – though had I known I might have proposed 'Upon this *rock* will I build my church'. Oh, never mind. They all seem to enjoy themselves, especially during the periods announced as PRAISE, when the drums and guitars thump monotonously away as the congregation endlessly repeats banal incantations of adoration and joy. My own message, about the spiritual benefits of silence, seem rather beside the point. However, when I have finished, one of the clergy generously calls for a period of contemplation. Peeking at my watch I reckon it lasts all of thirty-five seconds.

July 26th

Sylvia and I restore the balance by attending Quaker meeting at Marazion – a three-hundred-year-old meeting-house just inland from St Michael's Mount. It is full of cosy Quakers dying for a chat at the close of worship, but instead we have to hurry home to feed a lunch party called to show off our new recruit. Cold leg of lamb, gooseberry fool, Shropshire Blue cheese and Cornish Yarg, and cider. It went on for ever like one of those Sunday lunches in France, while the cats fought over the lamb bones.

July 27th–31st

A week of pleasant trivialities. The world outside (according to the BBC) is dancing itself into a frenzy over the Attorney General's attempts to muzzle Peter Wright the Spycatcher; and the clumsy efforts of the United States Navy to cut a dash in the Persian Gulf. But the lead story in our local paper *The Cornishman* is about a man who made one hundred obscene telephone calls to the lady operator on the Penzance police station switchboard – which I should have thought was teasing the tiger. Most of the rest of the paper, as usual in the summer, concerns sewage on the beach.

An expedition to the Duchy of Cornwall oyster farm at Porth Navas, which you get to via Constantine, which you get to via Gweek, via Helston. It is a lush and wooded landscape over there, where you drive through green tunnels down to sheltered creeks, quite unlike the windswept harshness of our Penwith peninsula. I get the feeling that you need at least a small cabin cruiser and a background in business to belong in those parts. Constantine, which was once a mining village, has an arts and crafts cooperative and a village store with a huge wine department which could trump anything in Hampstead or Highgate.

The oyster farm always plays hard to get. You ring them up in advance to find when they'll be open, and when you arrive carefully to time they've all set sail with the tide, 'because we ran out of mussels'. We strike lucky at our second call and come away with oysters, mussels and clams, which keep us happy for the next couple of days.

Then it's Ann's Day. Ann is an artist friend of Sylvia's. The bottom has fallen out of her house in Camberwell – quite literally – so she has sold the wreckage for what she could get and bought what must surely once have been the vicarage in Gwithian, between St Ives and Camborne. I regard this with some apprehension because although I am extremely fond of Ann she lives in the midst of a perpetual tornado, the serene centre of total chaos, and I can see us getting sucked into it. Fortunately we are at the wrong end of the transfer to be involved in the packing and departure of Ann's possessions from London, but we hang about in Gwithian awaiting their arrival – which doesn't happen. Eventually it transpires that a) Ann's handbag got stolen at the crucial moment and b) the rented van got stopped by the police for overloading and a 3½-ton truck had to be substituted.

This was to be driven by Ann's theatrical daughter Didi, but turned out to be so massive that she had to remove both hands from the steering wheel in order to change gear, which was tricky on things like roundabouts. Didi next recruited a male ballet-dancer to change gear for her – at which he was quite good, but being a ballet dancer dared not risk his dainty body actually shifting the furniture. For this, yet another young man was enlisted. Ann eventually arrives with a lorry, two cars and a retinue of four volunteers. The ballet dancer, worn out with gear-changing, retires to the beach to sunbathe.

To complete the week, our daughter Jennet arrives from London for the first encounter with her niece and namesake, now aged one month. They show every sign of liking one another. My only reservation about the baby is that, so far, it shows no sign of a sense of humour. Is there, I wonder, some rule of thumb like 'walk at one, talk at two, laugh at Grandfather's jokes at three'?

More uproar in the Gulf about the massacre of hundreds of Iranian pilgrims by the Saudis at Mecca. The Ayatollah proclaims an official 'Day of Hatred' when everyone in Teheran will pour into the streets and have a spontaneously organised mass hate against the Saudis, the Kuwaitis, the Iraqis, the Americans, the French and of course the Israelis. Quite an idea. British trade unions, already familiar with the Day of Action (when everyone docs nothing) might try the occasional Day of Hatred against Mrs Thatcher or the Coal Board. Arthur Scargill could pop off to Teheran and take lessons in hating from the Ayatollah.

An American lady who visits us for tea at Carfury prophesies the imminent outbreak of World War Three. Being a firm disbeliever in the world's ending during my lifetime, I say everyone ought to back off and keep calm. It is better to accept some casualties at the hands of the fanatics rather than go lashing out in revenge.

Talking of danger spots – CTVC have now come up with provisional dates for completing our homeless film, in the Philippines of all places. Next to Sri Lanka they could hardly have picked a less stable country for us to work in. But I shall only take this seriously once I'm through immigration in Manila, not a moment before.

August 6th

Up to London by train to hold Jennet's hand during her next spell of chemotherapy – the admirable Ed being out of town on a gliding course. The next two or three days are doubly upsetting – there's a kind of cultural wrench anyway between Cornwall and London and then back to Cornwall again; and this is the first time I have seen our daughter through the full two-day torture. I won't dwell on the details. She is incredibly gutsy about it, but ends up looking like the victim of a Gestapo interrogation. Ed turns up at the last minute and behaves with a lovely tough tenderness.

August 12th

We are back at Carfury and I am sadder, no wiser, cheered at least to realise that we have had three or four weeks of excellent weather in Cornwall, while London has sulked under a wet, grey blanket. There is a family of buzzards across the valley: parents and one child. One of the adults drifts high overhead while the other two patrol the landscape uttering shrill mews to scare the game. Buzzards are back at last because – I'm told – the rabbit population is recovering from myxomatosis and so there's enough food to support their predators again. We take a picnic down to Trevail Mill valley, near Towednack, and find more buzzards there. On the rocks off the coast we count a dozen seals, lolling luxuriously and yawning with the sheer boredom of being fat and well-fed.

August 15th

We coast down the hill to New Mill and dine with Phil and Melissa Budden at the Old Post Office (every other house in these parts seems to have been something it no longer is – Sunday School, Chapel, Mission or Mill). Apart from anything else it is a very delicious meal with most agreeable company – Margo Maeckelberghe, the painter, with her doctor husband Willi, and Prof Charles Thomas, the Cornish scholar, and his wife Jessica Mann. Melissa is an agreeably self-made woman. Texan by birth, an American degree in Eng. Lit., came to England and qualified as a nurse, then a bookshop in Richmond with a small publishing house on the side, in the course of which she built up a large collection of books by or about women, not aggressively feminist but important enough in its field to be without rival on this side of the Atlantic. Melissa has housed it in a snug granite barn next to her house, complete with residential accommodation for a visiting scholar or two. Not at all what you would expect to find in an obscure Land's End hamlet. But then, obscure Land's End hamlets seem to be attracting more and more unexpected characters these days. Can the Cornish survive it?

August 16th

We stuff spring bulbs into nooks and crannies about our stony Cornish garden, then pack up to return to London. Weatherwise it's been a pretty good summer in Penwith and besides giving Diana's calves a few weeks of better grazing than she has at Camborne, the field behind the Sunday School yields a good cut of hay.

August 24th

A jolly lady called Jo – friend of a friend – moves in to house-sit and tend the cats. The suitcase opens its jaws once more and swallows a wad of washable tropical clothing – we are off to Jamaica for a week. The pretext is the editorial board meeting of the *International Christian Digest*, of which I am an unlikely member. Unlikely not only because I am a notoriously bad committeeman but because the *Digest* is really the child of the Methodist churches of the USA and Great Britain. While I like the radical activism of Methodists I don't really share their sacramental theology and verbose form of worship. However, in launching this international review of theology last year the Methodists thought it good to appoint what I suspect was meant to be a figurehead board of holy people, in the expectation they would assemble once a year, utter blessings upon the endeavour and leave the American staff, in Nashville, Tennessee, to get on with it. Our one reward was to have fares and expenses paid annually to some agreeable meeting-place like Montego Bay or Geneva.

But to the well-controlled embarrassment of the editorial side, we boardsters have turned out to be a great deal more interfering than expected. Far from nodding things through, we have been tearing them apart. The net has not been cast wide 'enough for material, we complain, and the magazine is far too lavishly produced and laid out. It looks more like a glossy company report than a serious intellectual review. That, at least, has been modified in the latest issue.

No point in spinning out yet another grumble about the dreary intercontinental bus-ride from Gatwick to Montego Bay by way of Miami. This time it is an American airline which I shall call Confidential since I do not wish to get involved in an argument with its public relations department as a result of stating here that it is one of the most incompetent and amateur airlines it has been my misfortune to get trapped on. The cabin staff seemed to be vacationing students who know each other all too well and throw lovely parties for themselves in the galleys while the passengers thirst and starve.

Sylvia and I promise ourselves that at least we shall be able to buy copies of the banned book *Spycatcher* as we change flights in Miami. But although we find four different bookstalls in the infernal circles of its terminal building (abandon hope all ye who enter there – especially if you don't speak Spanish), they all stock the same dozen titles, of which *Spycatcher* is not one. It is bad enough having to plod through the rituals of immigrating into the United States only to emigrate a couple of hours later, but apparently the Constitution of the USA requires it.

The captain of our next flight – which I don't mind saying was Eastern – fancies himself as a folksy philosopher. Instead of the routine 'We are now flying at 20,000 feet . . .' he tells us that 'Our trusty bird is moseying along 20,000 feet above Mother Earth. Me and my crew will be doing our durn'dest to find you Montego Bay somewhere down there – either that or somewhere just as dee-sirable.' The American passengers smile indulgently. The British look embarrassed. Incidentally, British travellers are far bolshier than Americans. Brits demand things and complain when they don't get them, stage little protest demonstrations and occasionally lose their tempers. Americans suffer everything blandly, as if the one great sin were *not* to 'have a good day'.

Montego Bay is No Problem. Everything in Jamaica is supposed to be No Problem, which ought to suit the Americans. It's a sort of easy-going form of OK. You order a beer (the Red Stripe is excellent when served very cold) and the waiter says 'No problem' and vanishes for hours. You ask a porter to shift your bags. 'No problem' he cries, holding out a hand for the tip – and leaves them just where they are. Over the driver's seat in the bus is a handwritten sign proclaiming: 'Tipping this driver is NO PROBLEM'. Tipping, in other words, is a universal nuisance in Jamaica.

August 25th

Still, it's a nice hotel, if a bit luxurious for us austere theologians. The usual American accommodation, each bedroom equipped with *two* huge double beds which seem to hint Why not bring a friend and *his* wife?

We have a balcony looking out onto the Caribbean over a terrace planted with palm trees and incorporating an open-air restaurant and swimming pool. It is all just like the films or a Kodacoloured brochure, right down to the beach girls. Oh golly! the beach girls! with their bikinied breasts and airbrushed tummies tanned to every shade from a discreet apricot to richest mahogany. None of your Palethorpe's pinko-grey. Nor your saucy French toplessness, either. American girls (which they mostly are) have this peculiar way of looking beautiful without implying they know what sex is about. As if to underline this, lots of them go about in two and threes together, unaccompanied by men. Let us think about something else. Food, for example.

Well, it's not bad. There's the great American breakfast, greater even than the North British businessman's breakfast, with lashings of tropical fruit and juice, eggs, bacon, pancakes with maple syrup, baskets of croissants, muffins, 'Danish', and coffee, coffee, coffee. A snackish lunch off the grill. And in the evening a 'character' buffet which might be seafood, traditional Jamaican dishes (curried goat is No Problem, I find) or – one evening – steak and lobster tails, cutely labelled Surf 'n Turf.

Lots of black people at the hotel – yuppies and professional folk from the American east and middle west. And handsome young honeymooners.

But it is far too hot, into the nineties and very humid. The sun squeezes the energy out of you by midday. Sylvia's routine is to bathe after breakfast – the sea is so warm you could stay in it all day without a shiver – then to paint in the shade of the palms until lunch and then take refuge in the airconditioned bedroom till sunset, to the distress of the room maid who thinks everyone ought to be out on the beach getting brown. The Australian message about skin cancer does not seem to have reached America. I am luckier in a way because the board is shut up in a cool committee room all day and only gets let out for supper.

August 26–28th

Well, who have we got on this board? First there is Richard Peck, the maddeningly self-effacing editor from Nashville, and Brian Thornton, his deputy on the British side. The British can't really throw much editorial weight about because 90% of the circulation is in the States and the American Methodists have put half-a-million dollars into launching the *Digest*. Then from London there's me and Pauline Webb. Pauline is a tough white-haired Methodist from the missionary and ecumenical staff of her church, just retired from being organiser of religious broadcasting for the BBC World Service.

From the States we have Joe Lowery, Martin Luther King's successor in the Southern Christian Leadership Conference ('I'm no theologian. I'm just a preacher-man'), and we have Father Charles Curran, presently being roasted by the Vatican for holding naughty views on contraception. We used to have Hans Küng, the even naughtier Catholic theologian from Tübingen, with whom I had some invigorating scuffles last year; but he seems to have lost interest and hasn't come this year. Nor have we got our Korean lady member. Nor Desmond Tutu. Nor an Australian bishop. Nor a mysterious Zairean called Masamba ma Mpolo who doesn't answer letters. But we do have Ulises Hernandez, a Mexican Methodist. And above all we have Dr Philip Potter, a massive black Methodist from the Caribbean and former Secretary General of the World Council of Churches, at whose invitation we are gathered here in Jamaica.

Philip I know quite well from covering conferences of the WCC when I was BBC religious affairs correspondent. I am afraid he did not always appreciate my coverage when he heard it coming back on the air. There is, I know, a case to be made for stressing racism, capitalism and neo-colonialism as prime concerns for the Christian churches today; but there is also a case against that. I for one have never personally owned a slave, exploited an African or lorded it over a colony, and resent the implication that somehow I still furtively do all three. But Philip insists on seeing things differently. He has – justifiably, I am sure he would claim – a large racial chip on his shoulder, and you can tell by the sinister chuckle in his throat when it has been touched. Pauline, who has known and worked with him far longer than I and certainly shares his concerns, devotes much care to picking up the pieces when the chip falls off. On the other hand, she has a chip of her own about women's rights, and much of our discussion swings to and fro between black theology and feminist theology. Nobody speaks up for gay theology, child theology, animal theology – and only me, I suppose, for lay theology.

I get rather tired of hearing the others open up their remarks with 'Speaking as a trained theologian . . .' as if that were some guarantee of infallibility.

Philip, as our chairman, rules our business with firmness if not exactly economy – subjects come up two or three times over, sometimes without much relevance to the running of the *Digest*. As, for example, do we believe the magazine reflects adequately the sense that the world is proceeding to its own destruction? Well, I don't think the world is, but I'm too scared of Philip to argue with him. I wait hopefully for the scheduled debate on the Ordained Ministry, on which I had done some considerable homework. But when we get to it, Philip declares it is 'too difficult' for us and ordains a debate entitled Doing Theology Today.

Now I know this is a fashionable catch-phrase in the trade; but after an evening's contemplation I come to the conclusion that if it means anything it can only be *acting upon* theology today and try to bring it down to a personal level of how do I apply my beliefs about the nature and will of God to my services towards others. It turns out, however, that the trained theologians see the doing of theology as the talking of theology – notably black and feminist theology. But to my mind we couldn't begin to *do* it until we got up and left that room. To be frank, I was peeved at being deprived of my chance to have a go at ordained Ministry. Maybe Philip guessed what I would have said. For while I can understand people valuing the services of a professional leader-teacher-pastor, I can't go along with the bit about magic powers being conferred by the laying-on of hands, nor with people offering *themselves* for ordination (instead of being called by the congregation), and don't see how the whole thing squares with JC's injunction against His apostles calling themselves Rabbi, Father or Master (see Matthew Ch. 23). All of which is heretically Quaker, but there you are. I suppose medical doctors would feel much the same about a self-taught herbalist.

Oh well, we did a thorough job on the magazine, at least – urging the editors to cut down on their lead time (at present it's taking up to a year to get an item into print) and to shake up the network of contributors, many of whom haven't sent in a word yet. Poor things, the editors are grotesquely understaffed and overworked, and we urged them to take on more staff. But it's highly unlikely the backers will spare the money for that on the present circulation.

August 29th–31st

Most of the Board steam off for other destinations. Sylvia and I stay on for a few days' vacation. Had Jennet not fallen ill this is when we would have flown up to Philadelphia and the Quakers of Pendle Hill.

We bathe, eat, snooze, read and paint. In the abstract it seems like a good idea to go on lots of tours into the island, but practically it's too darn hot. All we manage is a drive along the north coast to a waterfall, and a pleasant hour drifting down the Martha Rae River on a bamboo raft. The water is clear, the banks cool and lushly jungled though curiously bereft of wild life. Our total sightings for the afternoon are one bedraggled crow and three high-altitude vultures – plus half-a-dozen Coca Cola vendors lying in ambush here and there. Sylvia, who remembers Australia in terms of kookaburras, wombats and spiny echidnas, is greatly disappointed. So is the raftsman who tries to sell us a particularly useless ornamental gourd for the equivalent of five pounds. I explain that we are English, not American, and that the English are noted for being mean. 'But I want you to have something to remember Jamaica by!' he cries. 'I shall remember it perfectly well without an ornamental gourd,' I say firmly. 'Yeh – you're a *reel* Englishman all right,' he sneers. That I can understand, but most Jamaican patois is wholly unintelligible to us – not a consonant in earshot.

The hotel compound is guarded as if we were a summit conference. Stroll a hundred yards away from the terrace and you encounter uniformed men with Dobermanns on leash. Once I look up from my papers and see a patrol of four policemen with riot guns sauntering through the palms. I'm told the mugging rate among tourists once got so bad that hotel owners could ring up the police and they'd send over a helicopter that would shoot anything that moved after dark. Beside the road outside the little town of Falmouth the authorities have left a couple of smashed up smugglers' aircraft as a warning, but they still flutter in by night from the mainland. One clever entrepreneur built a grand avenue through the sugar cane fields and announced it was to be the axis of an estate of holiday villas. The villas never got built but the avenue made a splendid runway for several months.

I can't pretend to have my finger on the pulse of Jamaican public opinion – Montego Bay is about as representative as Miami Beach is of America – but judging from my breakfast paper *The Daily Gleaner*, the island's concern with racism is peculiarly introspective. The Sunday edition publishes an interesting guide to degrees of blackness:

MULATTO child of white man and negress.
SAMBO child of mulatto and negro.
QUADROON child of mulatto woman and white man.
MUSTEE child of quadroon woman and white man.
MUSTIPHINI child of Mustee and white man.
QUINTROON child of mustiphini and white man.
OCTOROON child of quintroon and white man.

After that, you pass as white. Apparently it's unthinkable that the woman should ever be other than black, or at least one didn't talk about it in slave days.

The black cat has been tossed among the pigeons lately by none other than Marcus Garvey Junior. M.G. Senior was notable in the '20s for his Back to Africa movement, though the US imprisoned and then deported him for financial fraud. Jamaica has since rehabilitated his memory and Marcus Jr is busy trying to revive some of his father's racial doctrines, especially that you're not black unless you're *really* black – down with the leadership of the café-au-laity! So far as Marcus Jr is concerned Jamaican Premier Edward Seaga, who is of Syrian extraction, is 'a white man' and his rival Michael Manley is 'a deputy white'. Being faintly brown isn't good enough. A counter-attack is now launched in *The Gleaner* arguing that cultural values and speech count, too. Your skin could be as black as coal but if you were a Fabian Socialist and spoke like an Oxford graduate, you'd be morally brown. On the other hand you could be a goat-eating, reggae-singing, patois-speaking octoroon and qualify as black at heart. Thus does racism, black as well as white, strangle itself in the end with its own nonsense.

Marcus Jr, I gather, created further uproar among the trendy leftists of London by telling one of their gatherings that he was disgusted to find British black leaders (few of whom would pass his test of blackness at all) espousing such causes as gay and lesbian rights. Homosexuality, he told them, was an abomination and a violation of African moral and cultural values. There was a huge booing and much walking out. The moral here is that you can't please all the progressives all of the time.

September 1st

And so we leave sweaty Jamaica with our quota of rum and carved wooden birds.

When I die, they will find Miami written on my heart – or maybe Confidential Airlines. For a start, Eastern get us to Miami an hour late, leaving us less than an hour to change planes. We immigrate and emigrate at a desperate jog, yell at the porters to transfer our bags, and arrive at the Confidential desk to find chaos. The flight has been overbooked and they are offering free seats on some later plane to anyone who will sell back their reservation. We are the very last two passengers to be allowed aboard. Then we sit on the ground for an hour and a half while engineers patch a hole in the wing. Then we have the usual cattle-boat crossing. Then, arrived at Gatwick – no luggage. We stand by the carousel watching the same bags go round and round becoming more and more familiar, but not ours. Some are badly damaged, but we wouldn't mind even that if they were *our* suitcases. Some are still parading past, unclaimed, after an hour; could it be that their owners, now in Barcelona, are watching ours go by with equal despair? Among the orphans is one of those baskets used for keeping cobras in. But the ropes have slipped, the lid has gone, the basket is – empty.

We report tearfully to the desk of an outfit called Gatwick Handling which is a sort of Salvation Army of the lost luggage world. They take down details of our runaway darlings, offer reassurance and tell us to 'phone after two days if nothing turns up on our doorstep.

Gloomily home, wondering is this the end of a faithful friendship between Man and Suitcase?

Purrful reunion with the cats who have given Jo much pleasure. She, in return, has filled the house with little posies in unexpected corners. For days after, we are discovering *that* egg-cup stuffed with geraniums in the lavatory, or *that* jug overflowing with heliopsis by the telephone. Nothing much seems to have happened otherwise.

September 3rd

No suitcases. Gatwick Handling confess they have nothing to report, though they have cast many a telex upon the waters. 'When do I abandon hope?' I ask. 'We *never* abandon hope,' they say, as if affirming the power of prayer. 'Call again in two days' time.'

On the wireless Sylvia and I listen to Graham Leonard, Bishop of London, in Anthony Clare's Psychiatrist's Chair. Quite fascinating and confirms much of what I suspected. Yes, he admits, he does have strong feelings and a volcanic temper which he strives to control. He wants to get his way by virtue of reason, not force of personality. This annoys Sylvia: 'Doesn't he think other people will be able to stand up to him? Why doesn't he let himself go?' My own reading is that this is an aggressive man who is terrified of what might happen if he acted spontaneously. Then he makes the revealing admission that if he saw a woman at the eucharistic altar his instinct would be 'to embrace her'. And he doesn't much care for women lecturers for the same distracting reason. He seems to have got it figured out that women do womanly things and men do manly things and he feels terribly confused and threatened if their functions become blurred. I think he must have had the same sort of warped public-school upbringing that I did: Woman as the alarming and mysterious Mother goddess who can only be put in her place by rape (which you mustn't, of course). All this talk of the separate roles of the sexes and of the priest standing in for the male Christ is so Freudian it gives me the creeps. Clare never publishes his own analysis of his victims, but I would dearly love to read his notes on this one.

September 4th

One by one, Sylvia's friends check in to see if she's back for the winter. As one of the world's best listeners she has an unwritten register of people who unburden themselves to her at irregular intervals. This is no good for her efforts to get on with her art work, but it does have the benefit of driving me out of my downstairs armchair and up into my study to get on with this diary. How is it that women are so *kind* to one another while men will hardly ask each other for a match?

It is Jennet's chemotherapy day. As all too often, the hospital keeps her sitting in terror for hours before sticking in the poisonous drip. Worse still, the prognosis is not good. Unpleasant things have been growing when they ought to be disappearing. We end the day rather depressed. Even the patient Ed is gloomy, one of his tropical fish having committed suicide by leaping out of its tank.

September 5th

But now for the good news: the salvationists of Gatwick turn up with our suitcases, smiling shyly but refusing to say where they've been. I tell the van driver he's the most welcome visitor we've had since Santa Claus. I tip him handsomely. 'Thanks,' he says, 'you never know if they're going to shout for joy or burst into tears.'

Jennet comes round escorted by Ed. It looks as if she will have to give up full-time work as a graphic designer and find part-time jobs. A number of her dream projects will have to be scaled down. Sylvia, practical as ever, pre-scribes a kitten.

September 6th

Rum gives me gout. I haven't had an attack for two or three years but I have now and it's agony. Like toothache, it is absurd to be at the mercy of one tiny appendage – a giant laid low by a thorn. But I am helpless in the grip of it. It does not help that the world regards gout as a joke and cries, 'Gad sir! Been at the port again?'

As if to take my mind off it Jennet and Ed turn up with *two* tortoiseshell Burmese, neutered females ten months old and named provisionally (though surely this can't last) Stalin and Trotsky. We lock our own cats in the bedroom and play with the newcomers. They have lean oriental bodies, tails like pipecleaners and Picasso faces. They purr vigorously and converse in husky, sexy voices. It is immediately clear that cat therapy is exactly what Jennet needs.

September 7th

Gout still hell. CTVC rings up to say that Martin the director and Ginny the production secretary have been out in Manila exploring the project, were there during the latest attempted coup and didn't notice a thing. They reckon the Philippines are No Problem, so we shall fly out on the 17th and return on the 24th. Sylvia is not convinced ('I don't want my husband's life at risk as well as my daughter's . . .') but I am so bored with the whole thing already that I shall be glad to get it over.

A letter comes from the BBC asking if I would like to present four programmes about Martin Luther King next year. He had a dream, you remember, that 'my four little children will one day live in a nation where they will not be judged by the colour of their skin but by the content of their character'. Well, what has become of those four? Yes, I say, I would like to go back to America and do that. Provided it doesn't mean changing planes in Miami. No, I'm assured – Atlanta.

September 9th

No good pretending – summer is over, amidst much wailing and gnashing from the farmers, especially those who have gone into wheat in a big way. After last year's glut our apple crop is a washout, though the plums have been better than expected. Chestnuts are beginning to hail down – our resident squirrel is going crazy trying to bury them all – and the plane trees along the lane are shedding their bark untidily.

I hobble off to see my dentist, who is Armenian. This is the second time in my life I have had an Armenian dentist, having had one in Beirut twenty-five years ago. He is painless and very good at his job but keeps pressing me to install an expensive bridge in my upper right-hand jaw. There is a gap there that doesn't show from outside but is, I fear, intruding a slight hiss into my speech which is not good for broadcasting.

Things fall apart . . . For some reason, or maybe none, the streets around are full of excavations by the gas and water men. Springs bubble out of the pavements, guard-lights twinkle in the night. But no longer do they unload little huts and lighted braziers beside which old men sit reading the *Daily Mirror* and frying sausages on shovels. They used to; I remember it well.

September 14th

An armoured brigade of road-menders with tanks and heavy drills has moved onto the roundabout fifty yards from our house. They exchange fire with another road-mending project not far away, and the uproar sounds like the Battle of the Somme.

Jennet rings with a slightly more optimistic interpretation of last week's body-scan. Her consultant, a woman cancer specialist, is briskly determined not only to drive the beast back into its cage but to shoot it dead there once and for all. Morale rallies in response, especially as Jennet now has a two weeks' pause in her treatment.

Martin the TV director calls confirming that we leave on the 17th for Manila, though he promises Sylvia that if there is another commotion out there in the meantime, he will cancel. I'm an old enough hand to know how to keep out of trouble, but I'm still doubtful we shall actually go.

In between such distractions I manage to write the article on Ordained Ministry for the *International Christian Digest* and post it off to Nashville, Tennessee. My message being that the so-called Apostolic Succession has little if anything to do with the Apostles, I can't imagine this being wildly popular with our largely clerical readership.

A wordy lady from the BBC in Birmingham telephones in the evening to ask will I join with John Timpson in recording a two-hour Christmas morning chat show for Radio 4? There will be bells, carols, readings, interviews with drop-in guests . . . It will be good to see John again – we worked together in Alexandra Palace more than twenty years ago – so I say yes. Though my heart sinks a bit every time Christmas or Easter comes round and I know I shall be asked to do a holy bit. 'But not *too* holy, please, old boy . . .' Is there anything new to be said about Christmas?

September 17th

I get in a terrible mess what with trying simultaneously to interview two bishops *and* leave for the Philippines. Eventually stagger down the path to the taxi, dragging the suitcase and sobbing, 'But I'm too *old* for this!'

'Go off and enjoy it!' says Sylvia.

At Gatwick I am reunited with the CTVC crew – not quite the same one as in Lusaka. Martin, the handsome, slightly enigmatic director; Stuart, the electronics engineer; and Malcolm, the tall, beaky sound-man who is crazy about cats – these are all the same. But we have a new cameraman in Brian, and a charming production secretary called Ginny. An agreeable bunch that knows its business and works hard.

To the alarm of some we are flying Philippine Airlines. But in my experience the service on these Asian outfits – Malaysian, Singapore, Thai, anyway – is excellent and so it proves with Philippines. It helps that we are flying business class: the seats are wider, the leg-room limitless, the food appetising and served by delicious honey-coloured ladies who are efficient without bullying. Frankfurt, Dubai, Bangkok, rise up to meet us and fall away again quite painlessly.

September 18th–23rd

Manila. The Hotel Kublai Khan, alias Hyatt.

I was here more than twenty years ago for a meeting of a now-collapsed American alliance called the Southeast Asia Treaty Organisation. It always was a crazy country, a mixture of Asia, Polynesia, Spain and America jumbled together on more than a thousand steamy islands. Life is fairly dangerous – 'Please check your gun in at the desk before proceeding' is a standard sign in Manila office buildings – but the people work hard, determined to make a living in spite of the soldiers and politicians on their backs. Interesting that Filipinos hardly ever describe themselves as *unemployed* – they are *self-employed*, trying to get by somehow, even if it means going off to the Middle East or Western Europe on low wages. On weekdays the squatter slums are almost empty of layabouts: everyone seems to be out looking for something to do, something to buy or sell, even if it is single cigarettes to drivers caught in traffic jams. The fabulous jeepneys – jeeps turned into mini-buses – roar up and down the avenues six abreast, decorated like gipsy caravans. Some have Rolls-Royce radiators bolted on, others have Cadillac bumpers or rear light assemblies from deceased limousines. Their bonnets glitter with brass bedstead knobs and chromium-plated horses, while every available panel bears some incantation like *Pennies from Heaven, Look before*

you Leap, Jesus Loves Me or *Small but Terrible*. Popular sur-
realism is part of the culture.

It also applies to Filipino names. The Cardinal's name is
Sin, and there is a radio priest called Father Bong. There's
a rebel colonel known as Gringo and politicians with
names like Joker Arroyo, Leander Alexander, Hermogenes
Concepcion. But the dominant personality in our brief career
here is a small mad Filipino nun called Sister Veronica who
presides over the housing project we are to videotape. Sister
Veronica hurtles through the security barriers at the airport
and throws herself upon us squawking, 'He is coming! He
is coming tomorrow! A big British minister to meet our
President!' And when we fail to be impressed, 'Your big
minister – very important! You will see, you will see
your big minister.' We say politely that we'll give him
a miss, however big (actually he turns out to be some
minor functionary from the House of Lords who makes a
preposterous statement about how firmly rooted democracy
is in the Philippines these days): we've come to Manila for
the housing. But the mad nun keeps after us, rearranging the
same words over and over again until we are tempted to swat
her with the camera tripod. And she is going to be our escort
for the next five days.

Wherever we go, Sister Veronica – five-foot-nothing – is
hopping alongside plucking at our elbows like a manic duck
crying, 'Look – from here you can see all Metro-Manila!
All Metro-Manila from here you can see! See, from here,
Metro-Manila – all of it!' Gradually it dawns upon us that she
interprets our lack of enthusiasm as a sign of dimwittedness;
that she doesn't think we understand English very well.

What she is doing is worthy enough, though not entirely
purged of power mania. By diligent use of her pecking-to-
death technique she has bullied the Catholic church of the
Saarland in Germany to give her the money for two modest
housing estates for the respectably poor (the abjectly poor
have to look elsewhere), whom she is now teaching to

97

improve their properties by their own efforts and to govern their own communities. There is no doubt that Sister Veronica is a formidable trouble-shooter, chaser-up of contractors and cutter of red tape. Not surprisingly her residents, all hand-picked Catholics, have elected her president of their housing association. Just as unsurprisingly, the Cardinal has come to the conclusion she is empire-building beyond the vocations of a nun and is trying to prise her from office. But Sister Veronica is one jump ahead: she has a private housing foundation of her own up her sleeve which she operates from an apartment block in downtown Manila left to her by her mother. Chastity I can believe, but poverty and obedience don't seem to come naturally to our heroine.

How is this possible? We get a whiff of the answer after the first morning's filming, when it is announced that we shall be lunching at the home of Sister Veronica's sister in the mountains. After a drive through the suburbs we find ourselves being admitted by an armed guard into a walled compound, patrolled by Alsatians, in the midst of which stands a villa which would not have been out of place in Beverley Hills. Veronica is very well connected. Her brother-in-law is 'an agent for business. He was very close to Marcos, but no trouble there now.' The sister is out shopping, but in the lofty entrance-hall there is an oil portrait of her in the style of Mrs Marcos.

Lunch is laid out on the terrace and servants gather round fanning the food with fly-whisks. There is fish. What kind, I enquire? 'Special fish,' says Veronica confidently. A day later there is more fish. 'Different fish,' she asserts. They are equally good and much to be preferred to the 'authentic Filipino dishes' I am foolish enough to order in a restaurant one evening. The pigs' trotters ('Knockout Knuckles') have been overcooked and allowed to go lukewarm, and the Golden Snails are disgusting, swimming in what appears to be Indian ink. My stomach rocks on its heels and then recovers its balance with a wry smile. Veteran of gastronomic ghastliness from Cairo to Cambodia, it takes more than a lukewarm knuckle to knock it out. The best food in Manila is Thai. And the local beer – San Miguel – is excellent very cold.

Veronica doesn't miss a trick when it comes to publicity. She intervenes in every interview, sidles into every shot, even turning up in a game of basket-ball when we thought we had decoyed her out of the scene. It is excessively hot and humid and our tempers wear thin as the day progresses, but Veronica never tires, is immune to our snaps and snarls. She keeps luring us towards a strip of derelict scrubland where she wants to build yet another colony of her empire: 'You will go back to London and raise funds for me – then I call it London Peace Village – TV Peace Village – Priestland Peace Village. What you want, I call it. You will raise funds, yes?' We'll mention it, we say. I should add we've already agreed a healthy fee for her cooperation.

Back at the Hotel Kublai Khan, with its polished marble floors and gliding cocktail waitresses, I punch up the BBC World Service on my Japanese shortwave and listen to the news. Manila, it seems, is on the verge of revolution. Leander Alexander has been shot in the street, troops are manning road-blocks everywhere – anxious relatives ring up members of the crew from London asking if we are safe. But we haven't heard a single bang or met a single soldier. It's not that the BBC is telling lies but, as I well remember from my own days on the job, a reporter goes where the trouble is and most of us are where it isn't. Manila is so vast and sprawling that it can absorb a small civil war without 95% of the population being aware of it.

Which is not to say that the makings of something serious aren't present. Marcos and his missus spent borrowed money until 60% of the budget was earmarked for interest on foreign loans. Much of the money seems to have gone on building grandiose complexes for banking, for sport, culture, administration, designed to impress other Third World governments without doing much good for the ordinary Filipinos. The huge Financial Centre, for example, stands glittering on the edge of Manila Bay – empty.

The Philippines, like Sri Lanka, are lush enough for nobody to need to starve. But they are also so disjointed as to make an impossible nation to govern – over a thousand islands offering dozens of opportunities for local barons and warlords to set themselves up. A central government needs efficient armed forces, but when the government is not efficient the forces get fed up and either refuse to go hunting rebels or stage rebellions of their own. The textbooks say the answer is land reform to win over the peasants. But is is one thing to issue proclamations in Manila – quite another to get them carried out in the thousand islands. Landlords know a thing or two about frustrating land reform, in any case.

We have hired an airconditioned minibus to drive around in with all our equipment. (Videotape, though it brings the advantage of enabling you to see what you have shot without having to wait for processing, encumbers you with quite as much apparatus as film does). One day the driver announces that his employer, the travel agent, is throwing a party at the Ambassador Hotel to celebrate his birthday and we are all invited. There will be a show, he says, with girls. The driver then hands out vouchers entitling us all to a 20% discount at a so-called drive-in motel (or knocking-shop) offering 'Ingenious love-seat in every room – Special mirror effects – Imaginative bathrooms'. The TV crew, a virtuous bunch of lads compared with some I have worked with, shudder and think of England. No thanks, they say, but it would be churlish to decline the party, so we go to that.

It turns out to be almost as appalling. Our host, who resembles a mountain of Turkish delight draped in silken chemise and harem pants – 'as camp as a row of pink tents' to quote our director – presses us into a booth from which we can observe his equally monstrous transvestite lover miming to music. He/she is dressed like the madame of some brothel in Basra, in black velvet slashed and strapped with gold to allow great rolls of writhing flesh to peep through. Fellini would have been proud of it, but it is too much for the boys (and one girl) from the Churches' Television Centre, and after a couple of San Miguels we flee. 'You missed the girls,' said the driver reproachfully next morning, 'they take all their clothes off. Also you miss the lady with the snake.' As I said to Sylvia when I left home, I'm too old for this.

Taking Sunday off we go out of town on a river trip which beats the Jamaican experience hollow. Squatting in dugout canoes we are paddled and manhandled for two hours through a deep, jungle-clad gorge at the top of which is a spectacular waterfall. We paddle right through this into a cave where we bathe, and then shoot the rapids down again. Highly recommended, though you have to be prepared to get very wet.

On my last morning I manage to get in a little sightseeing in what's left of old Spanish Manila, known as Intramuros ('within the walls'). Really this amounts to some walls and two or three churches going back to the seventeenth century, one of which contains a contentedly fusty collection of holy images from the colonial period. Filipino Catholicism is heavily Mariolatrous – most of the houses I've been into have a garish corner shrine to the Virgin with a little figure of Christ crawling at her feet. In Spanish times they seem to have been unusually devoted, also, to St Roque (or Roch or Rocco) presumably because he was the patron of plague victims. He is always shown coyly lifting the hem of his kilt to reveal a sore on his left knee; and often there is a dog reaching up to lick it. Actually I have nothing against saints. Far from it.

Then my taxi driver insists upon taking me to see something he swears I will see nowhere else in the world. It turns out to be the Chinese cemetery: street after street of marble town-houses, perfectly kept and furnished, like holiday homes in some expensive seaside resort, but occupied by nobody save the dead. 'Nowhere else in the world!' insisted the taxi-man, and sulked when I told him that, making allowances for the architecture, it was just like the City of the Dead in Cairo and served much the same purpose.

Come to think of it, ancestor-worship is not an implausible form of religion. Christianity builds God up so high that it's hard to believe he can pay individual attention to billions and billions of people ('Dear Creature . . .' the heavenly circulars might begin). But if one's parents and grandparents have survived at all, what more natural than that they should still be taking an interest in the family – provided, of course, the family is still taking an interest in them. It's not all that different from saints. I admit this is unscriptural, unprotestant and unQuaker, but I wouldn't blame people for using it as a ladder to cross the gap between us down here and Him up there.

I manage to escape Manila without a farewell fund-raising appeal from the Mad Nun. Laden with painted wooden birds as presents for the family, I settle down to a twenty-hour night back across Asia, the Middle East and Europe to meet the sunrise at Gatwick. This time the suitcase keeps to heel.

September 25th

In the ten seconds between waking and opening my eyes I wonder am I a) in an aeroplane b) in Manila c) in Jamaica d) in London e) in Carfury? A quick peep says London. An exploratory toe says No Sylvia. I remember she has already left for Cornwall to help Diana with arrangements for the baby's christening – in particular to mass-produce sausage rolls. I throw out the tropical laundry from Manila, stuff in my churchgoing suit and the carved wooden birds, and stagger off to Paddington for the Penzance train. A rustic progress in the restaurant car in company with a doctor who turns out to be a cancer specialist, but even this is more agreeable than trying to converse with the man across the aisle – an advertising man who insists that British television is the *worst* in the world and the BBC needs destroying because it denies the people their choice – by which he means all the lovely commercials he could fit into its air time. Would that he could have seen Philippines Television, with its dawn-to-midnight evangelists begging for money so they can come back next week to beg for more money. One that sticks in my memory was particularly hot on the heresy that we are *all* God's children. Unless we have chosen Christ we are the *Devil's* children, he cried – yes, sweet little children and little old ladies all going home to Hell because they did not know Jee-zuss! Why, there were some folks who said God was like a mighty mountain we were all climbing by different routes. (And here I warmed to this preacher, because it's an image I often use myself.) But the Bible didn't say anything about no dumb mountain! God ain't no stoopid mountain! There just ain't no top to Almighty God! And the Reverend Hellfire went on to compare God, in some detail, to a clock radio. If you don't follow the instructions in the book, He cain't do a thing for you! There's only ONE WAY! May God in his mercy keep my grand-daughter free from the Reverend Hellfire and his like and jolly Jack Adman and *his* like.

We slide into Mount's Bay on time, and Sylvia is waiting with the senile Renault. The clan is gathering.

September 27th

And it gathers, most creditably, in full strength at Kehelland Methodist Church: Sylvia and me, Jennet and Ed, Andreas and Sally, Oliver and Natasha, Diana and Raymond, plus, of course, the star hereinafter known as Jennet

Natasha, now almost three months old. I am glad to report that the cross-little-old-man side of her stayed away from the christening and that gurgling innocence held sway. Though, as a result, she did fail one of the tests of folk religion by failing to cry when the water was splashed over her; so I suppose the Devil is still in her.

Of all the rites of passage marked by the church, baptism is still the folksiest and in many ways the richest – full of all that imagery based upon water and signifying rebirth, washing away sin, salvation from the flood et cetera. Parents, no matter how irreligious, don't seem to feel their children are properly launched into life without this touch of magic (a no-no word sacramentally) – presumably a survival from the days when people believed that a baby unbaptised went to Hell. What cruelty! I am told that Limbo is really a haven of mercy, though it is going out of favour theologically.

The actual naming of the child, which many people regard as the main purpose of the operation, is of relatively little importance in the eyes of the Church; though in the early days it must have been of vast significance when a pagan convert deliberately chose a *Christian* name – usually that of a saint or martyr whose protection was being sought. Today name-choosing is a mixture of fashion, class-consciousness and family favourites. No working-class child could possibly be called Jennet Natasha, the first name coming from *The Lady's not for Burning* and the second having exotic Russian overtones. No daughter of our class could possibly be called Sharon, Yvonne or Charlene; just as no son could be called Darren, Wallace or Trevor. Julian, Roger and James are nice middle-class names, with Susan, Charlotte and Anne for girls. Gerald (an ugly name of Teutonic descent) may not be popular but it's guaranteed non-working-class.

The Church, however, grits its teeth and confers almost any name ordered. Elvis if you insist, though I've heard of parents being sent away to think again about Lulu and

Ringo. It doesn't matter a lot because the name isn't legally binding anyway.

So here we are in this little Methodist church, taking part in a normal Sunday morning service but with a difference: two babies to be baptised, our daughter's and another member of the congregation's. There was a time, especially among well-to-do Anglicans, when christenings were private affairs, furtively done in the afternoon; but nowadays the feeling is – rightly – that if the ceremony means anything it includes welcoming the baby into the wider family of the Church and so the congregation ought to be there in witness.

And so it was, beaming happily in its Sunday best. Methodism is the true People's Church of Cornwall, the church of the fishermen and tinners who love to sing like their cousins the Welsh. So we had lots of lusty hymns with repeated refrains, long extempore prayers, and a minister who talked to his people instead of holding a private conversation with his prayer-book. Cornish born, he was, darkly handsome and with white tabs at his throat like a young Wesley.

Each baby, as it was baptised, was paraded up and down the aisle in the minister's arms, much as a rabbi parades the scrolls of the Law for everyone to admire.

And then off home to the sausage rolls and sandwiches and cider – with orange juice for those whose Methodist principles have not slipped to the extent of admitting alcohol. The six khaki ducks who normally occupy the front garden are shut up in their duck-house; and the sheep-dog Kally is pushed out at the back to gaze mournfully through the kitchen window at the fun inside. About half the company is local; the other half has come two or three hundred miles at no small expense, giving the lie to the theory that the extended family doesn't exist any more. I suppose we would never have had such a mob of our own if Sylvia had not been one of *seven* brothers and sisters. But it seems sad to me that families today are so tiny and see so little of each other.

Cue for small sermon: It is simplistic to blame the whole situation on government policy. For years it's been fashionable to decry formal marriage and family life as repressive, reactionary. Marxists, feminists, gay liberationists, champions of birth control and of abortion and divorce on demand have all thrown stones at the conventional pattern. The liberal-minded centre hasn't done much to resist the trend. But neither has government. For all the talk of Victorian Values, little if anything has been done to encourage the stability of families or to cushion them against the battering they have to take from an increasingly complex and competitive society. It's not a matter of asking government to subsidise breeding – though that is the case in parts of continental Europe, where the term Family Policy is respectable political currency. One might at least hope our government would cease to penalise it.

I suppose social engineering is now out of fashion. The left still talks about class interests and the right responds with the primacy of the individual. There is nothing in between. When the National Campaign for the Family (for whom I did a paper recently – hence this sermon) wrote to the Prime Minister urging her to take a personal concern in the matter, it got back a letter saying the government did not regard the concept of Family Policy as conducive to clear thinking – that it would be wrong to promote the interests of the family in situations that conflicted with the best interests of individuals. How would that sound, I wonder, to the abandoned mother of two small children whose father has pushed off to pursue his own best interests? The best interest of any individual, especially in early life, lies in a stable family. But then, as a born-again grandfather, I would believe that, wouldn't I?

Back to London.

October 6–8th

Whatever else, this is the Year of the Hole-in-the-ground.

Our gas meter having been doubly condemned, first for being out of date and second for being illegally encased in a cupboard, the authorities now quite sensibly propose to install it on the outer wall of the house where it can be read by the inspector whether we are at home or not. The Americans have always done this, which is probably why the British have up to now regarded it as a foreign eccentricity. But one thing leads to another, and British Gas have decided it cannot be done unless a) they relay the entire branch from the mains in the street to our back door, and b) I myself do the necessary carpentry to expose the guilty meter, since 'Laying hands on woodwork is not our function'. I manage to lay hands on it quite easily. Tearing things down I find no trouble. Putting them back again is another matter.

On day one, two sweaty men who look like off-duty football hooligans arrive and dig trial holes around the house. They confess themselves baffled. Where has the gas pipe gone? Out in the street they sink two more trial shafts to no avail, and come the dusk are obliged to cordon them off with red-and-white striped barriers.

On day two it rains heavily. The men knock off and the holes fill up with water. Chunks of mud like chewing gum sneak into the house when no one is looking, and muddy paw-prints make it all too clear what the cats get up to when our backs are turned. Sylvia, though never an obsessive housewife, is in despair.

On day three, British Gas zap us with everything they've got. A sinister machine like a geiger counter sits in the garden uttering the sort of bleeps that heavy lorries do when going into reverse. A road drill is brought in to sink yet more holes, and an explosive thumper to fill them in again. A new, neater man arrives to bore a hole through the kitchen wall and braze pipes together with a flame-thrower. Snakelike coils of yellow plastic pipe lie on the lawn. Suddenly it all falls into place. The bleeper finds out where the old pipe has gone, the plastic snake is pushed up the middle of it, the neat man fits it to the outdoor meter and we are back 'on stream'. Apart from some loose paving stones you would hardly know what chaos was reigning a few hours earlier. So congratulations and apologies to the hooligans, who have had to wrestle with London clay at its nastiest. I even manage to restore the devastated cupboard to its former shape, so that where the old meter lurked we can now store marmalade.

But on the cancer front the news is worse again. We may have to dig in for a grim winter. Sylvia is like a lioness defending her wounded cub against the hyenas of Death.

Talking of cats, Mi-Nyoo, the Burmese, who will be thirteen in January, is beginning to show the first signs of losing her ascendancy over Cadbury, the two-year-old Siamese. Cadbury is an ex-male, but very laid back. He didn't even notice when the vet de-balled him. His attitude to life is 'Cool, man, cool!', upon which he rolls over and displays his creamy paunch to be tickled. I've never known a cat which spent so much of its life upside down. Out-of-doors, he shows extreme caution and although a skilled dustbin raider, never gets into a fight. Knowing a wimp when she saw one, My-Nyoo intimidated him from the start; not so much with her teeth and claws but with a basilisk stare which could drive him off a sofa at twelve feet. No hungry generation was going to tread *her* down.

But of late Cadbury has started to throw his increasing weight around, getting in a crafty nip or swipe in passing. There was a spat in the studio just now, and the tufts of fur left under the table were not Siamese.

October 9th

A good way of brightening up your life, I find, is to have your spectacles serviced. World looking drab? Mind unable to grasp what you're reading? TV programmes getting worse and worse? Pop along to your oculist for a test and it could be that you are merely going blind. My eye-lady, Kussoom Vadgama, says it's not as bad as that. I don't even need new glasses. I just need the old ones polishing and tightening up. And after three days stumbling miserably with an obsolete pair on my nose, back come my bi-focals and the world is transformed. Out comes the sun, writers pull themselves together, television sparkles once more. Through a glass brightly.

October 11–12th

I am booked to do the Monday morning Thought for the Day, but in spite of the glasses am totally out of significant thoughts. Half-way through a convivial Sunday lunch with old foreign correspondent pals Louis Heren and Roger Toulmin I get the message 'Loch Ness Monster' followed by the quotation, 'There go the ships: and there is that Leviathan whom thou hast made to take his pastime therein . . .' And from then on it's a pushover. For there indeed go the ships, or rather a line of motorboats strung out across the loch with their echo-sounders bleeping away to reveal SOMETHING lurking in the depths. The bookmakers are shortening their odds against the monster.

There are five references to Leviathan in the Old Testament, including one whole chapter of Job that begins, 'Canst thou draw out Leviathan with an hook? . . . He maketh the deep to boil like a pot . . . He maketh a path to shine after him . . .' Alas, I'm afraid it's about a crocodile, and if the Loch Ness monster isn't going to disappoint us, it's got to be something more unusual than that or a big halibut. What the public needs is something prehistoric that will make fools of the scientists and renew our hope that there are Abominable Snowmen in the Himalayas and dinosaurs deep in the Congo.

Personally I hope there are – and that we'll never be able to prove it. For I tremble to think what will happen if we do find Nessie alive. No question, under the present regime, of making it a National Treasure: if we can't afford to subsidise a dinosaur like the University of Oxford we certainly can't throw money at some overgrown Scottish newt. So it will be up to the tourist industry to make Nessie pay its way. The beast will have to be brought to the surface and taught tricks. Its sex life will have to be rigorously researched and artificial insemination employed so that the species will flourish as vigorously as, say, the giant panda.

Heaven forbid. If there is something down there, it is one of God's last secrets left upon earth and I think He's entitled to keep one or two.

I'm afraid there will be complaints that, as a Thought for the Day, this is somewhat frivolous. But on a Monday morning it makes *me* feel better.

Monday evening, Oliver turns up and borrows the money I had been hoping to spend on a new suit. Well, at my age, why bother with a new suit?

October 13th

Lunch in town with BBC producer and John Timpson – a 'working lunch' to make plans for our Christmas morning show. John has now retired to a prepared entrenchment in his native Norfolk and gives the impression of not wanting

to emerge from it very often. After years and years of handling all comers to his studio with impartial courtesy, he
now allows himself some most emphatic dislikes: at least
three darlings of the listening public, proposed as guests,
are given no shrift whatever and firmly vetoed. Shire horses
will not drag their names from me.

October 14th

Another lunch in town, this time with my agent John
Parker and a publisher's lady who has a proposition. A
bit coffee-tablish, but not urgent, and it might be as well
to make sure of the income for the year after next.

Coming home I knock out a review for *The Ham. &
High*. of Trevor-Roper's latest book of seventeenth-century
historical essays. I feared it was going to be dry as dust until,
on the second or third page, I encountered a marvellous
event known as 'The Great Fart in the Parliament House of
1610'. Exactly what it was is never disclosed, but it inspired
at least two poets of the day – one of them Ben Jonson – and
provides T-R with one of the very few clues about Nicholas
Hill, a more than usually obscure philosopher of the period.
He may, it seems, have been the grey eminence behind 'Basset's Plot', the fantasy of a pirate named Robert Basset who
tried to create Utopia on Lundy Island – only nobody paid
any attention, so he lost heart and ran away. So did Hill,
though T-R admits it may have been some other Hill.
Never mind: it is a most elegant academic conjuring trick. A
later essay about Laud's activities at Oxford and Cambridge
makes C.P. Snow's stories of university politics sound quite
innocent. I first encountered Trevor-Roper when he used to
examine us history specialists at Charterhouse. His waspish-
ness and gusto for the language are only a little less than they
were forty years ago.

October 15th

With rather less enthusiasm I review Eric James's biography of John (*Honest to God*) Robinson, which tells me
rather more than I wanted to know about him. It wasn't,
I suppose, his fault that the press made such a sniggering
picnic of his evidence in support of *Lady Chatterley's Lover*
– though it was unclever, and surely unnecessary of him to
walk into that in the first place. Only in theologically back-
ward England, with its theologically illiterate media, would
Honest to God itself have been regarded as revolutionary. At
best, John Robinson was an old-fashioned Victorian radical
born out of his time; but the Englishman and -woman in
the pew – when they bother to sit in it at all – expect
the theology of their childhood hymn-books. The most
interesting work Robinson did was on bringing forward
the dating of the gospels and arguing the priority of St
John's. I met him a couple of times at Cambridge,
where he looked unhappy. It is a pretty place, but
remote; and snobbish, cliquey Trinity was exactly the
wrong college anyway. They should have found him a
billet at Oxford.

October 16th

Wake soon after four in the morning to the roaring of
a gale – in fact, a hurricane. It is stripping the leaves
off the big chestnut across the road, whose branches are
flailing in a panic to get away. At half past four the street
lights go out. The mains-operated radio is dead, but my
little battery set tells me most of south and southeast
England has been blacked out and the main roads and
railways into London are all blocked by fallen trees or
masonry. The BBC is running on emergency generators.

So is the Weather Bureau which admits sheepishly that it hardly knew what had hit it. Sylvia and I lie in bed with the house getting cold around us, except for the freezer which is presumably thawing its supplies. The doorbell (another battery gadget) calls me downstairs to find Sally Birch from two doors along saying a big branch from the chestnut has split off, blocking the road and narrowly missing our car. Can I come and help?

So I dress quickly, grab a rather futile handsaw and plunge into the storm to find the Birch family already hacking away heartily with an armoury of puny weapons with which they manage to reopen most of the Lane. Naturally, none of the drivers waiting impatiently to get through bothers to thank them. Splendid folk, the Birches, who never stand idly by when everyone else is doing precisely that. Rosemary, the mother, and three of the children, put up warning barriers, collect the debris in piles, scorn the usual attitude of 'leave it to the Council'.

By noon the gale is tapering off. Miraculously, the four lofty poplars that stand at the bottom of the garden like a tea clipper in full sail are still standing.

Woozy with sleeplessness, I try to review yet another of Isaaman's eccentric choices: David Spanier on Gambling. This, it seems, is either a substitute for sex (which suggests an alarmingly unstable sex-life on the part of those who believe that) or a genetic reflection of the chanciness of the universe. I must say I think it's a mixture of greed and superstition – the belief that one can get rich for nothing if only one can identify that lucky moment waiting in the stars. But then I have not got the temperament to make a successful and disciplined gambler. Spanier, whom I remember as a *Times* correspondent in Washington, evidently has. But apart from him, what a worthless lot are the gamblers he describes: Lownes, Aspinall, Lord Lucan, Frank Sinatra . . . I wouldn't play Snakes and Ladders with Sinatra.

October 18th

Having bought a highly effective Swedish saw for six pounds, I decide to miss Quaker Meeting and spend the morning cutting back the fallen chestnut still further and acquiring some logs for the fire. For some possibly atavistic reason connected with violence, felling trees and sawing logs is one of the few physical activities I enjoy. A pity I can't find something more creative. However, I produce forty logs before lunch, which I cook myself because Sylvia has gone into orbit taking Sunday school, dashing off to nurse Jennet, visiting her sister Edith, ringing up Diana to see how things are in Cornwall. One haystack blown over, otherwise the complaint there is rain rather than wind.

It's Thought for the Day again tomorrow. I had planned to do something metaphysical about the hurricane, but Sylvia reports that Meeting was all about the Week of Prayer for World Peace, so I switch to that, saying it may sound naive but *somebody's* got to carry the peace banner or it will be compromised out of existence.

In the evening I get down to the Sunday papers. There is much baying for the blood of weather forecasters, now seen as the chortling charleys of the day before the deluge. But what could we have done if they *had* got it right? Duck? There are lots of fallen-tree photographs. Kew Gardens have been tragically decimated. But again, how could an early warning have helped?

The critics seem to have liked Greenaway's film *The Belly of an Architect,* and so did Sylvia and I, which is gratifying – I had to be dragged moaning and groaning, as usual, to the Screen on Haverstock Hill. The story turned on two or three cleverly combined axles, but apart from that – what a pleasure to see really deep-focus photography again, and huge, noble, head-on compositions: television with its narrow frame and dodging zoom lens has practically destroyed both. The bursts of music, too, are formidable. They would be far less impressive over a small-scale sound system at home.

The gale has managed to downgrade the news from the Commonwealth Conference in Vancouver, where everyone was out of step except our Maggie. Mind you, she has a point or two even if they were scored below the diplomatic belt. I don't much care for crying hypocrisy – but there are gross examples of it on all sides among the Commonwealth brothers and sisters. The Ghandian Empire, now on the march in Ceylon, is bidding fair to replace the old Indian Empire. Pluralistic democracy is hardly a *specialité* of the African *maison*. And does one not detect a certain zest for apartheid and racism in Fiji? But I suppose one is not meant to attend such conferences to wash other people's dirty linen. The Lady is really no lady at all. Also she seems to have been very badly advised as to the mood of all the other Commonwealth countries, or she would have cooked up and announced some meaningless 'new measures' against the South Africans. They would, of course, have had little effect without a naval blockade and ultimately a Third Boer War, which is where the logic of the Commonwealth is leading.

The net effect of sanctions so far has been to encourage South African industry to stand on its own feet, to increase the Anglo support for Mr Botha and to invigorate the Afrikaaner extreme right who are a very sinister bunch indeed. On the basis of my own limited experience I can see no hope for South Africa in the face of the relentless multiplication of young unemployed blacks. The situation levels out for a while, then crashes, levels out again, then crashes deeper towards total chaos by the end of the century. To whose advantage? In the meantime Mrs T's disdain infuriates the coloured Commonwealth (which is in no position to bell the cat itself), and this in turn encourages a sly form of racism among the new Tories.

Our next-door neighbour complains tactfully that our cats are making a luncheon club of his dustbins. I am ashamed of their squalid plundering. They have pedigrees out of the Bible: Peniralt Picasso begat Lokiplum Charman who begat True Grit who begat Aduam el Bonzo who begat Cadbury of Carfury . . . But what sort of a society is this in which next door's garbage is more appetising than premium-grade *Whiskas*?

October 20th

So 1987 is to go down not only as the Year of the Big Blow but the Year of the Great Crash. Wall Street, Sydney, Tokyo, Hong Kong, London tumble after one another to slash billions off the values of their shares – thus proving to me that those values always were illusory. One felt a growing detachment between the economy and the market, and I suppose this is what they call a 'correction'; only when the world's exchanges are all wired up to one another, what used to take weeks now happens overnight. Apparently computers are now programmed to *sell* automatically. This is what you get for treating investment as a computer game.

If I remember rightly, we were told during the recent election campaign that the British economy was getting stronger and stronger. The common folk were enticed into handing over their savings for shares in it. True, each prospectus carried a government health warning – but is *this* what Mrs T. had in mind, a mass lesson in the vanity of greed? Maybe she is, after all, a secret Puritan. What a comfort to think that while she's away visiting Mark in Texas, we are safe in the hands of that relaxed duo Willie Whitelaw and Nigel Lawson.

Meanwhile I see that William Rees-Mogg has returned happily to preaching the virtues of the gold standard. I do hope he has had the foresight to convert those extremely boring volumes in his antiquarian bookshop into bullion.

October 21st

The market is feeling better now, thank you. Not entirely recovered by any means, and it's had a nasty shock; but everyone's blaming a) the computers and b) the Americans and saying there's nothing really wrong with us – a sack of potatoes is still a sack of potatoes (in fact potatoes are probably worth more because of the soggy weather).

Jacqueline du Pré is dead, alas. BBC TV plays a film of her yearning performance of the Elgar concerto with her husband Daniel Barenboim conducting. One senses the lovely conspiracy between them as she flashes him a quick grin that exactly matches the phrase she has just played; and then her head and shoulders return to their deep participation in Elgar's rage and sorrow. Her command of technique and intonation is so secure that, while she is playing, you can pension off all the usual anxieties that lurk while a virtuoso piece is being played. She once told me that one reason she had come to terms with being unable to play any more was that, in any case, she had come to the end of the repertoire: there wasn't much more to be done except pass on the knowledge as best she could to the next generation. But I'd like to think of her in Heaven, being coached by Elgar as to what he *really* meant. May they play on together, in joy.

October 22nd

In the evening we go to the private view of the Camden Annual – this year richly sponsored as the 1987 Constable Art Competition, with prizes totalling an undreamed-of £2,350. The Sorpresa restaurant in Hampstead has donated a first prize of £1,000, which is hardly to be believed. Sylvia goes along rather gloomily, having had only one print out of four accepted, and that not her best. But when we discover that only 115 pictures have been hung out of 1,400 submitted, and that she is virtually the only one of the older generation (dating back to the 1950s) to be shown, we cheer up. As a whole it is a reactionary selection: a high level of academic competence, soberly representational, little that reaches out to grab you. Wyeth and Cezanne are here by proxy. The American abstractionists might never have been born, except for one small glowing corner with three canvases in it. The young, it seems, are going back to the '30s and earlier while we oldies are stuck in the swinging '60s and '70s.

October 23rd

Obscure letter from a listener in Cardiff: There are six dioceses in the Church in Wales (Disestablished). Can I tell him how many there would have to be for the Bishop of St David's to become Archbishop automatically instead of by election? This is so recondite that it seems the perfect excuse for a walk across Hampstead Heath and a couple of pints in Jack Straw's Castle. One has to be totally obsessed by church etiquette to think such a question even worth asking. Actually it isn't: it simply Does Not Apply.

October 24th

A theological afternoon with the Quakers. We hear a talk on Jesus and the future of Quakerism by Richard Rowntree, the object of which is to smoke us out of our holes and get us to reveal how 'Christian' we feel the Society really is. Richard is on the committee which is revising *The Advices & Queries* – which are as close as Quakers get to an equivalent of the *Thirty-nine Articles* – and is obviously under pressure from trendier Friends to de-emphasise Christ and lean towards Universalism. Our particular meeting is broad-minded towards other faiths but, I sense, would not be happy to stop calling itself Christian and using the language of Christianity, if only as a set of tools with which to work. I'm afraid I put on rather a song and dance about this, but Sylvia confines herself to serving up the Number One Hit Cake at the tea buffet – a Martha rather than a Mary (but you know who was more popular with the disciples).

October 25th

The gale-felled chestnut provides us with the first log fire of the autumn. Jennet, outwardly in good shape, comes to lunch and afterwards we stroll in Golder's Hill Park, which is crowded. People seem to feel more at home with a fence round them than they do let loose on the unconfined acres of Hampstead Heath. Many trees are down, but not always the ones you would expect. Some ancient, hollow monsters are still erect while a few yards away much younger and solider trees have fallen over revealing fatally shallow roots. I have to get home early to write my Thought for the Day, in which I try to be light-hearted about the inevitability of death.

October 27th

Up and down go the stock markets. I think I had better stop trying to write about them until it is over and I can say 'I would have told you so if you'd asked.' Tony Benn and the Fantastical Left have been holding a Soviet in Chesterfield, of all strange places – the town where even the church spire's warped. They at least can chortle over the imminent collapse of capitalism; but nothing so exciting will happen, I'm afraid. The embourgeoisement of Britain has gone too far. The Thatcherites have dug themselves in. Suburban values rule the land, and any attempt at revolutionary theatricals will be firmly suppressed. Already the Labour Party (Kinnock faction) is complaining that the BBC has been taken over by the right. It seems like yesterday that Norman Tebbit was saying it was a nest of lefties.

I am rung up by the *Daily Mail* and asked if I can do a piece on the cue of an interview Mrs T. has given to *Woman's Own* – or rather one tiny corner of the interview in which she upbraids the church for losing its moral authority over the nation. (That actually set in with World War One.) As a confused liberal I am unable to fake a *Daily Mail* line on this – thus forfeiting a few hundred pounds in fee. The one constructive idea I can offer is that if Mrs T. is dissatisfied with the nationalised church of England, the least she can do is to introduce competition into the faith market by allowing evangelists like Jimmy Falwell, Jim Bakker, Oral Roberts, et ceteri (strong moralists, every one of them) to buy time on our television in which to preach the gospel in all its rigour. Not that it need be limited to Americans. The Reverend Doctor Ian Paisley (alumnus of Bob Jones University, North Carolina) is a notable prophet of the air and would be glad to bring the nation's morals to heel. Must write to *The Times* about this. Have now done so.

October 29th

Times has so far ignored my helpful idea. Perhaps it will earn its keep elsewhere. I fear it is getting harder to find outlets for material which is even mildly disrespectful of Our Leader. One senses, even in oneself, a tendency to come to terms with her view of life – if only because one wants to stay in the forum and not shuffle off to the wilderness, muttering.

At least the Leaderene seems to have been thwarted in her design to make that Lord Young (not a proper lord, in my view) chairman of the Conservative Party as well as king of the Board of Trade or whatever it is called nowadays. Her manoeuvres achieved the scarcely imaginable effect of making people quite sorry for Norman Tebbit. I'm finding it difficult to define the new ruling class which is emerging. 'Bounders' is a little crude. It's a special-ised branch of the middle class which perhaps might be called the golfing class. Philistinism is an important factor. I read that Glasgow – a city which is trying hard to redeem itself – got chosen European Cultural City for 1989 and decided it would be appropriate to build itself a decent concert hall. Not only has the government declined to make any contri-bution towards the cost (you can imagine how the French or Germans would have responded) but it has forbidden the city council to raise a loan upon penalty of rate-capping. But then, by voting Labour so perversely, the Scots have shown themselves unfit for such a luxury. Give them a concert hall and they would probably race whippets in it.

Got up feeling glum on account of a pressing invitation to deliver yet another funeral address next week. Straight to the dentist, who tries to install a dainty piece of engin-eering in my mouth; but it won't fit. Not his fault, but after an hour I stagger out muttering, 'Ve haff vays of making you squawk!'

Dinner at Ealing Vicarage with Michael Saward, a not-too-triumphal evangelical. I bow before the rushing might wind of the born again and shelter in the palpable holiness of a fellow guest, the Rev. Ron Swan, who is going to be vicar of Harrow-on-the-Hill. Being an Anglican priest is a bit like being a bank manager: some are generous, some are narrow, all are dreaming of transfer to a bigger and better branch by the sea or in the country. How many times have I heard the wistful murmur, 'All I want now is a nice little residential canonry somewhere in the West Country . . .', though not from these two, I hasten to add.

October 30th

Must go down as the golden day of this year. Jennet appears on the doorstep, fresh from a scanner-reading at the Royal Free, and announces 'I'm clear!', and bursts into tears. The cancer has suddenly given up and gone, just as we were preparing ourselves for another round of torment – even for the worst. It seems that though stubborn traces of the tumour were still visible after six months of treatment, they were in fact tottering ruins which collapsed soon after. Jennet will have to be monitored closely for months and years to come. The treatment has greatly weakened her resistance to normal infections. But for the second time, the hyenas have been driven off and she has life ahead of her. God be thanked for His mercy, and I climb the hill to St Jude's to kneel and thank Him. Why not to the Quaker Meeting House? Partly atavism, I suppose. Anyway, the Meeting House is locked.

This evening, Sylvia and I sit and stare at one another, inexpressibly glad but somehow like exhausted soldiers who have worked themselves up for yet another campaign, only to be told that peace has broken out. But glory, glory, hallelujah.

November 1st

Quaker Meeting becomes a Meeting to Give Thanks. Two members just recovered from serious injury are welcomed back, while Sylvia and I relate the good news of Jennet and thank all our friends the Friends for their prayers. How frail we are, but grateful for every day.

The Sunday papers are more than usually interesting, for a change. There is a general feeling that the final crisis of capitalism is *not* round the corner. Certainly the Russians are not celebrating it, and Mr Gorbachev looks rather shakier than the chairman of the Stock Exchange does. The rugger-playing Fijians, now that nobody's looking, are altering the rules so that the Indians never get the ball. A stern Methodist decree has gone out to the Hindus: 'No picnics or jollity on Sundays'. Meanwhile the monarchist *Sunday Telegraph* has one story saying people ought to stop gossiping about the Prince of Wales's marriage, and another story telling us what the gossip is. Heaven save us from a republic. Mrs T. (who is said to get on the Queen's nerves as well as mine) would probably install Lord Young as President.

November 2nd

Off to Windsor Castle, where I am a member of the Council of St George's House, a kind of think-tank presided over by the Dean of St George's (Michael Mann) and actively patronised by Prince Philip. St George's House conducts stimulating courses for senior clergy and lord lieutenants of counties, and brainstorming weekends on subjects like Violence and Society, Science and Religion, Youth and Unemployment. There are lots of conference centres these days, some of them pretty grim and prep-school-like; but St George's is quite the poshest. The surroundings are incomparable (choral evensong is thrown in free), the food excellent, and – being where it is – the place attracts a high calibre of staff and participants. It also seems to be on a pretty sound financial footing.

His Royal Highness the Prince Philip Duke of Edinburgh and whatever ('Sir' is acceptable face-to-face) shows up and takes the lead. He is treated – and expects to be treated, I think – much as one would a rather bright retired admiral. Not for the first time I get seated at his table for lunch, and while I must respect the convention that one doesn't tell tales about such encounters, we get on fine with subjects like the Great Blow (why some trees fall down and others don't), the mutual antipathy of cranes and bitterns, and (from my side) Keats's opinion of Scotsmen, which was deplorably racist. *Nobody* mentions the Prince of Wales's marriage. I must say Edinburgh looks stunningly fit and lean for his age – indeed, for anyone fifteen years younger. But then he scarcely eats a thing and drinks nothing but water.

The Council passes a brisk afternoon discussing what to discuss in future. The rest must be silence.

November 3rd

I set out at 8 am to drive to Worthing, where I am to deliver this funeral address for the mother of an old friend. By ten past nine I have barely crossed the river, and by eleven I have to admit defeat. Hacking through London from north to south is too much. There isn't a hope of getting me to the crematorium on time. Then, of course, the phone boxes won't work, or deliver wrong numbers, or nobody's there to answer. It is a really disastrous morning. The only bright spot is that when I get home again, defeated, my agent calls to say he has rounded up a contract for 1989 and there's at least two years' work ahead.

An agency trying to flog time-share villas in Spain begins its computerised letter: 'You have been selected because your gracious life-style shows that you appreciate the best things of life . . .' How true! But who has been peeping?

The Times, by the way, has published my letter about allowing the American evangelists take over our moral leadership from the C. of E. George Engle enquires whether it is meant to be funny, but I don't think he follows this particular speciality.

November 5–8th

We go down to Cornwall by train, leaving the cats to be fed by neighbours. The pensioned-off Renault awaits us at Redruth. It's a pleasure not to have to drive, and our senior citizen cards make it cheap; but British Rail has played a dirty trick by denying the dining cars to any but first class passengers. Queueing for hamburgers at the buffet is not the same.

Carfury is in good order – so is our beloved granddaughter, who smiles and gurgles happily. I plant crocuses, see the builder about re-opening a window in the cowshed; we eat and sleep and read and walk and are grateful that Nothing Happens. Our local paper, *The Cornishman*, has the usual front-page story about sewage. Once before it reported solemnly that sewage was not something Penwith could sweep under the carpet. This time it quotes a member of the council as saying that his vote on the matter was 'a gut reaction'.

Riding back to London, the train comes literally to a grinding halt on the edge of Bodmin Moor. The guard comes down the train and explains that our diesel monster cannot get up the hill because of 'wet leaves on the track': however he has sent to Plymouth for help. A broom? No, yet another diesel monster which thumps onto the front an hour later but makes no difference. I think they must have got out the broom after that, because it is almost two hours before we get moving again. To cheer us up we are told there *might* be a buffet attached at Exeter, but of course it isn't and we get to Paddington very late and very cross. British Rail is so embarrassed about the leaves that the loudspeakers attribute our delay to something they call evasively 'failure of the set'. A plate on the side of the offending locomotive gives its name as FURIOUS.

November 9th

John Halkes, director of the Newlyn Orion Gallery, has asked me to open an exhibition he's put on at the Royal College of Art: a hundred paintings by various artists of the past century, inspired by the Penwith coastline. The object is to underline the National Trust campaign to save as much of it as possible from the developers. So I tell a few jokes, get a few laughs, and declare it open. As always at NT affairs, the eats and drinks are excellent.

The Trust is moping a bit at the way Land's End has become a rich man's capital gains plaything – it changed hands a few days ago at almost £7,000,000 – but then, Land's End is a fairly dreary place anyway; not a patch on Cape Cornwall, which was given to the Trust earlier this year by Heinz the Beans. And they've managed to buy the Foage Valley at Zennor, which will please Patrick Heron. Patrick isn't at the show, but cheerful old Terry Frost is.

November 10th

My Armenian dentist finally installs some bridge-work that fits. From the bill, it must have been designed by Fabergé.

November 11th

Remembrance Day, properly; though we are still aghast at the IRA bomb massacre that took place in Enniskillen last Sunday (I didn't record it at the time as we were mostly in that train).

I've had Ireland on my conscience ever since I developed one. Over the years I've got to know the island and love it and have many Irish friends of every denomination. I've usually found an occasion to go there every year and do what I can, through the churches, for reconciliation – if it's only a sermon or a seminar. As an Englishman I acknowledge our heavy debt as exploiters and oppressors and as beneficiaries of Irish Christianity and culture. For better or for worse, Britain would not be what it is without the Irish connection.

That connection cannot be easily broken off. It goes far deeper than mere military occupation. We can't walk out as casually as we did from, say, Palestine or Cyprus (not that 'decolonialisation' has much of a record as a bringer of peace and freedom). The ineluctable fact is that Ireland outflanks England to the west, and in strategic terms England-Wales-Scotland could never permit the Irish island to become a base for a continental rival like Spain, France, Germany or any successor. Pacifists like me deplore that approach, but it is one of the facts of power and it is why England encouraged Scottish settlement in Ireland centuries ago, and thus it is the origin of the Catholic Protestant divide.

Even so, it's not so easy to make a neat distinction between immigrant Scots and native Irish. The Celtic sagas tell of a rivalry between Ulster and the south going back two thousand years. Ulster was linked with Scotland even then. In more recent times, you find the so-called bandit country on the border was lawless three hundred years ago. The violence at Enniskillen simply repeats a pattern of great antiquity – read the historian A.T.Q. Stewart. Remove the

British troops and would anything change? I suppose the Ulster Defence Regiment would say they *are* British troops. Who's going to disarm them?

Northern Ireland is no more a religious issue than it is a colonial one. Two distinct communities have grown up in Ireland, each defining itself more distinctly by its history and traditions. Although one has taken the badge of Catholicism and the other that of Protestantism, the quarrel is not about theology at all – it is about territory and power. Either you are born a cowboy or you are born an Indian; there is no question of one side converting the other, nor of the two coming together in a single race. In Northern Ireland, the two interlock like separate pieces of a jigsaw puzzle, but they do not merge. The only factor that has ever brought an appearance of unity is domination.

I fear that the influence of religion in favour of reconciliation is very limited. Enniskillen produced an outpouring of truly Christian sentiments on every side. But we have heard this before. What happened to the Peace People of 1976? The men and women of the IRA are Christmas Christians at best – all the year round they are terrorists, and excommunication worries them no more than a black look from the parish priest. Once tasted, terrorism is as hard to give up as heroin. The penalties for defection are drastic, the rewards for loyalty are lucrative – it is a paid profession. To repent of terrorism is to deny an identity rich in heroism, against which the Church has very little to offer.

One thing that has saved Ireland from even worse bloodshed is the fact that the Protestant (or more properly Unionist) tradition is one of organised soldiering rather than guerrilla warfare. There *is* Unionist terrorism, but feeble compared with that of the Republicans, and easily penetrated. As a result, the Unionist community has had to stand and take casualties with quite extraordinary steadfastness. But it would be wrong to attribute this to Christian forgiveness, and even more wrong to think the withdrawal of British troops would bring the rapid establishment of a united and peaceful Ireland. Ireland is not a problem but a history. Ulster is quite capable of resurrecting Cromwell for itself.

There is the old Belfast joke, 'But are you a *Protestant* atheist or a *Catholic* atheist?' As each outrage fades away, the religious leaders tend to identify once more with their own communities and are coopted into their politics. England and its churchmen have written off Northern Ireland like a drunken country relative who has to be paid for but need not be visited. Scotland Yard seems to have the terrorists in check on this side of the water, and if they do bomb us occasionally, we too are used to taking casualties. Where Hitler failed, etc. . . . This entry must peter out in despair, illumined only by the bright spark of individual Christians who suffer great evil but refuse to curse the dark.

November 12th

I couldn't make it yesterday to the General Synod debate on Sin – they're against it, I gather, but don't want to upset the sinners. Which is a deplorably glib summing up because, reading the less superficial accounts in the press, members seem to have done rather well. The puritans demanded the excommunication of homosexuals – swiftly adding fornicators and adulterers to show they weren't narrow-minded – but the crafty bishops substituted a motion advocating equal measures of repentance and compassion, with a pinch of holiness for those who could manage it. An altogether practical Anglican compromise, and conducted with greater seriousness and decorum than the House of Commons would have shown.

What annoys me – as it did back in February when the synod debated women priests – is the synodical devotion to chasing cuckoos. This is not an important subject, and the church is not primarily a society for the virtuous, anyway. Where would it be without its gay vicars – or its fornicators and adulterers, I dare say? All the bishops I know devote a good deal of time to monitoring the morals of their clergy and it simply is not true that the country is being debauched by dog-collared sodomites. To put it pompously: I don't think this is the sort of thing that needs to be discussed in public. It's bad manners. You keep your nose out of my private life and I'll keep my nose out of yours. Or next year it will be 'Should Christians masturbate?'

The unspeakable *Sun* has the headline PULPIT POOFTERS CAN STAY.

November 13th

My video director Martin takes me off to Hackney to interview John Turner, a 'community architect', whose ideas we think will neatly round off our film about the homeless. I've now drafted a script in which I eschew despair and argue that the homeless of the Third World can do a remarkable job of helping themselves if only governments will give them half a chance. And actually it's easier for a Manila squatter to help himself up than it is for a single homeless family in London, because minimum acceptable standards are more readily attainable in the Philippines. To my pleasure, Turner (whose work I hadn't read before) heartily agrees and gives an interview underlining my conclusions.

Film scriptwriting is a demanding business because you daren't stray far from the pictures and to some extent are at their mercy. But the discipline becomes stimulating, like writing formal poetry. I shall be glad to see the end of it, nevertheless: it has dragged on too long, this film.

In the afternoon, 700 words for *Woman's Realm*, who ring up in a panic saying their Christmas number hasn't got any Christianity and could I supply something not too secular but not too pious. So I give them Incarnation for the Housewife, with a menacing coda about the double meaning of Advent.

November 14–15th

A quiet weekend, glory be! Pot up some bulbs for Christmas, but is the timing right? In past years my paper whites have been too early and my hyacinths too late.

I open an aerogramme from Chanchal Sarkar in Delhi – an acutely intelligent newspaperman who later became director of a sort of Indian Chatham House. He writes enthusiastically about a piece I did on the BBC World Service. Chanchal says he *used* to attend Third World committee meetings in London but lately they have switched to Stockholm 'because of the ethnic tilt'. I suppose this is his way of referring to South Africa and/or Heathrow beastliness to brown and black visitors. It would have been less coy to say 'racism'. 'Ethnic tilt' sounds as if Londoners had taken to wearing dashikis and eating Mexican food.

November 17th

Lunch at the BBC with Ronald Farrow of religious broadcasting who wants me to present a couple of programmes about next year's Lambeth Conference – less ambitious than what I had dreamed up with Chris Rees (who has vanished in a puff of smoke), but more practical. Chris and I saw ourselves dashing off to New Guinea with digital stereo, but Ron doubts if we can afford much more than a couple of second-class returns to Canterbury carrying a Uher mono recorder. Like most of the men in the department, he's getting ordained and has already conducted the funerals of both his parents. The two women producers in the office are thinking of holding a synod on The Role of the Laity in Religious Broadcasting (this is an esoteric joke).

Ron passes me on to Stephen Oliver, who wants me to interview Martin Luther King's family in Atlanta next February. And Stephen passes me on to Beverley McAinsh who wants me to do Thought for the Day (groan) on Mondays in December. None of which, being radio, will pay well, but it's all decent exposure. The last set of Thoughts has just yielded a big bag of fan mail, which is a reward in itself. They weren't, however, the Thoughts I originally wanted to think: I sent in three parables which Beverley said were so obscure she couldn't understand them. Hence the Loch Ness monster, etc.

Bought Christmas crackers.

November 19th

Last night there was a hideous fire disaster at King's Cross station. The top of an escalator burst into flames and destroyed thirty people. I rang up son Andreas who commutes that way every day. Fortunately he passed through two hours before it happened. Sylvia's brother Paul passed an hour before that. We've devised this enormously clever way of life, but when it goes wrong the result isn't just an accident – it's a disaster. A fatuous remark. Wouldn't do as a Thought for the Day. Thank God it wasn't my turn at the microphone. Still more selfishly, it's going to make getting around London by tube even worse, just as getting around by car was becoming impossible.

I spend the morning on a talk I have to give at St George's House on Sunday, at a weekend conference of external affairs directors of major British companies and multinationals. It's about the role of industry in helping the young. I don't know what I'm doing there – I know nothing about the subject – but they've asked for me and

I like the atmosphere and I may learn something. For want of any practical experience I'm talking about the importance of business setting a good example by observing high ethical standards. In other words, a little light moral theology.

Outside, there falls a melancholy drizzle. It thwarts Sylvia who has spent the past few days doing a series of particularly rugged sketches of fallen trees on Hampstead Heath. It impresses me, how so gentle a woman can produce such tough pictures – and they're getting tougher.

November 20th

Off to St George's for the weekend. At my friendly neighbourhood liquor store, where I call for spiritual reserves, I hear the story of the Cadillac hearse which has been parked a few yards from my house since April, chromium teeth at the front, shiny fins at the rear. Originally it had Californian number-plates but has now been re-registered in London as a private car. Just imagine: IT IS THE HEARSE THAT TOOK MARILYN MONROE ON HER LAST JOURNEY. Some of the neighbours have protested against its taking up residence amongst us, but I think it adds distinction and can hardly be called inappropriate, seeing the crematorium is just down the lane. With the ashes of Sigmund Freud and the Hollywood hearse, we shall soon be on the tourist schedules.

November 21st–22nd

It's one of the ground rules of St George's that discussions are off the record, not for publication. I'll say only that this conference has gathered an impressive bunch of people, especially Anne Jones the educationist, now with the Manpower Services Commission. Some excellent ideas came up. But I can't help worrying: how many of these people have actually got the clout with their employers to get them into action?

On Saturday afternoon we take a couple of hours off. I decide to walk down the hill into Windsor and buy some much-needed cat vitamins and visit the Madame Tussaud exhibition in the old railway station. Emerging from the cloisters I am enthusiastically snapped by a flock of Japanese tourists twittering 'Firreep! Firreep!' to one another. I do my best to look like the Duke of Edinburgh, but I doubt if it carries conviction.

The Victorian exhibition does and I recommend it thoroughly: Her Majesty in 1897 emerging from the Royal Train, inspecting a Guard of Honour, even rising mechanically from Her Throne to tell Her People how Very Kind they are. I left humming 'Land of Hope and Glory' and feeling Proud of the Empire. You can always tell when a show like this is good because nobody throws rubbish about. Well, one wouldn't in the presence of Queen Victoria.

Home to find roast pheasant on the table.

November 23rd

Having worked on Sunday I assume Monday is Tuesday and keep my appointment with CTVC at Bushey to make a trial recording of the sound track. Being only twenty-four hours early, they manage to fit me in. It works quite well and Barrie Allcott, the director, agrees to pay me some lovely MONEY which will pass rapidly to the Inland Revenue.

A strange place, CTVC: a country house in the Green Belt stuffed full of the most up-to-date television gear. Like several other mansions in the neighbourhood it gives one the impression of being something to do with Intelligence – but I don't *think* it is. It would make a good front, though, with all those bishops and dog-collars popping in and out for courses in how to be interviewed or how to deliver a Thought for

the Day. And all the time they are intercepting spy mes-
sages transmitted by enemy agents in the other suspicious
mansions outside Bushey.

November 24th

The diary says CTVC Bushey 10.30; but I ignore it.

November 25th

The diary says *Lunch at Synagogue 12.30*, so I go. The
Reform rabbi, Charles Emanuel, wants to discuss a brains
trust I am doing there in a fortnight's time with Laurence
Spicer of LBC and Clifford Longley of *The Times*. Clifford,
never much of a time-keeper, doesn't show up, but we have
a pleasant picnic of salad and fish-balls and chat broad-
mindedly about God and the awfulness of fundamentalism
in all faiths. If I ever leave the Quakers I shan't go over to
Rome; I think I'll turn Jewish. Reform, of course.

November 26th

Out of the blue, a letter from St Andrews University in Scotland offering me the honorary degree of Doctor of Divinity,
to be conferred next July. Frankly, nothing has pleased me so
much for ages. Civil honours have no appeal to me; but to be
taken seriously at last by such a highly reputable academic
community means something. I have a nasty feeling I may
have to sing for my supper by making a speech; nevertheless
I tell the Senate I shall be humbly grateful to accept. Sylvia
is impressed but warns me I mustn't strut around signing
myself Doctor. Her brother Bill, who actually *worked* for
his DD comes to dinner along with sister Edith – the retired

anaesthetist – and there is much family small-talk at which I am not much good.

November 27th

I write a heavily satirical piece about Christmas for the *Daily Mail* – no room at the inn because of picketing by catering workers, three kings in trouble at immigration, etc. It seems to please them, so I run off yet another Christmassy piece in case someone else needs it – a speculative investment that will pay off next year if it doesn't this year.

The hedges outside my study window are seething with wrens and the bare apple-branches with tits, so I replenish their basket of nuts. Looking up from my work to watch, I am alarmed to see my next-door neighbour Tom Sales wobbling at the top of a ladder from which he is attempting to saw off a bough from his prunus. I call from the window, 'Can I help?' for Tom has wonky hips. But 'No' he says, and I watch while he gets his saw pinched in the cut. So I have the perfect excuse to stop writing, get out my own saw and cut through from the opposite side, whereupon the branch falls neatly in the right place, Tom's saw is released and I enjoy a rare moment of glory as a practical man.

In the evening to the English National Opera for *The Barber of Seville*, though with some apprehension because it is a new Jonathan Miller production and I am suspicious he may have set it in Frank Cooper's marmalade factory in 1887 or perhaps a unisex hairdressing salon in present-day Golder's Green. Mercifully it has a pretty conventional romantic decor, and although Miller has tried to wedge in some references to the harlequinade, the singers manage to ignore this and we are able to enjoy the opera for itself. Della Jones as Rosina is quite brilliant – not a twiddle out of place.

November 29th

Sylvia and I 'sit up' as presiding elders at the Quaker Meeting
– not that our Meeting House has a platform for us to sit up
on. Anyhow it is our job to set the tone of the gathering, and
if anyone were to create a disturbance or harangue Friends
beyond their endurance it would be our job to restore order.
The classic put-down for over-long ministry is, 'Our Friend
has given us much to contemplate and I am sure the Meeting
would be grateful for a period of quiet now in which to consider it . . .' A quick glance round those attending suggests
it will not be necessary today, and it isn't. Indeed, after half
an hour of total silence I feel impelled to rise and encourage
Friends to utter. But it produces no result of any depth, so I
suppose the Spirit is busy elsewhere today. After Sylvia and I
have closed the Meeting by shaking hands, the children come
in bearing an Advent wreath with four candles, one of which
they light. Quakers lighting candles! It'll be incense next.

November 30th

Mass arrest of paederasts in Brent. Boys are said to have been
imported from as far away as Devon. I do not know what
to make of this epidemic of child abuse. For once nobody
is pretending it can all be blamed on television. Brent's
outbreak of paedophilia sounds like a locally organised vice
ring; but the goings-on in the northeast of England (now the
subject of a lengthy judicial enquiry) suggest something that
could be a feature of family life all over the country. It has
been suggested that a couple of over-zealous paediatricians
armed with some new and nasty diagnostic technique have
exaggerated the whole thing. But when telephone hot-lines
are set up and publicised, all too many victims call in.

What is to be done about it? Here am I writing pious

articles for the churches extolling family life, and the rose bush turns out to be riddled with worms. Children are pretty things, no doubt about it. But how can anyone who has loved a woman be drawn to a child in that way? And yet I have known some distinguished paederasts. Married ones, too. Cases for treatment – which they probably won't get, only to be abused themselves when they get into prison. The violent reactions of 'decent men' disguise the blind lust in us all. Why should women trust us?

December 1st

To Brown's Hotel in the evening to see Donald Coggan (Lord now, Archbishop that was) present the Collins Prize to Father Gerard Hughes for his lovely book *God of Surprises*. For once I tipped the winner, and the jacket bears the encomium 'One of the great books of spiritual guidance – *Gerald Priestland*'. But its greatness does not intimidate: it is wise and lucid and deeply human. Above all, a book to be *used* by people who find it hard to forgive themselves, the stumblers and agnostics who can hardly dare to believe that God is within them – which is good Quaker doctrine coming from a Jesuit. Father Gerard came and hugged me for saying as much in print and declared me 'the Pope of the unchurched', which had better not reach the Society of Friends. A gathering of agreeable religious folk – John Harriott and Shirley Duboulay, David Winter, Margaret Hebblethwaite, Mary Craig, David Edwards, etc. – all talking about what *they* are now pressing towards the bookshops. We are served tiny pieces of smoked salmon on toast. Collins's parties aren't what they used to be, nor are any publisher's. I can remember when champagne was *de rigueur*.

December 2nd

Yet another party – this time the Radio 4 Christmas beano in a fancy basement off Portland Place. Food much better than last night but plonk deplorable. In fact I hate these organised shouting matches under low ceilings; but to be honest I have to go to them to demonstrate that I am still alive and available. Want some famous names? Robert Robinson, Derek Cooper, Robin Day . . . Before all sensible conversation becomes impossible I have a pleasant chat with Laurie (*Cider with Rosie*) Lee. He tells me his wife has been out with the village undertaker probing the churchyard with a steel rod to find an empty plot to bury him in. But he doesn't look that far gone. (Note to my own survivors: Take me down the lane to the furnace, please. Then toss the cinders into the chasm between Carnello Cliff and the Long Rock.)

December 3rd

A great uproar in the Church over this year's *Crockford's* preface – anonymous as usual, though I suspect an Oxford academic of High Church sympathies. He pours scorn on the General Synod, which is easy sport. But then he goes on to accuse the Archb. of C. (Robert Runcie) of 'nailing his colours to the fence', discriminating against the Anglo-Catholics and the Evangelicals and packing the bench of bishops with Liberal cronies – liberalism being presented as some kind of way-out leftism rather than middle-of-the-road. And, of course, Runcie's Church is supposed to have gone soft on adultery, fornication and homosexuality.

Perhaps the shrewdest observation in the preface is that the best way to the top nowadays is to put in time with the BBC's religious broadcasting department, which Runcie used to monitor as chairman of the Central Religious Advisory Committee. I can think of five bishops and three deans who have come up through that, though I can't see it as a bad thing that a modern prelate should have some command of the electronic pulpit.

I hope and believe that Runcie will let it blow over. But the sinister thing is that *Crockford's* is now published by the C. of E. itself; and while Douglas Lovelock of the Church Commissioners denies all knowledge of the matter, Derek Pattinson, the pin-striped eminence of the Church House bureaucracy (and a High Churchman in sympathies) is maintaining a mountainous silence. Derek is out of the top drawer of the civil service and very close to the dreadful duo of John Gummer and Peter Bruinvels, Tory members of Synod. So one wonders whether a string has been pulled from as far away as Downing Street? Mrs T. and the golfing class have never forgiven Bob Runcie for failing to be triumphal after the Falklands, or for poking his nose into the inner cities, or for failing to take a firm stand against Sin. Dash it – why can't he behave like the Pope?

Meanwhile, the BBC is under fire as well for making radio programmes about the intelligence services and refusing to submit the scripts to the Attorney General for censorship. Though in fact the D Notice committee was kept informed and had no objection. The Attorney General slaps an injunction on the Corporation, which now finds itself unable to report what is said about the matter in the House of Commons, or even to name Peter Wright as the author of that well-known book *Spycatcher*. I don't mind the government looking ridiculous, but I resent it making the entire nation look like a troupe of clowns in a broken-down circus.

I don't know whether to ask my friends for *Crockford's* or *Spycatcher* for Christmas.

December 4th

Sylvia and I go out to an eight-seated Hampstead dinner-party – exactly the right size for my taste. In view of the government's sudden fondness for the law of confidentiality I had better be careful what I say, but here are a few gleanings from a rather high-grade field:

Pattinson is in the *Crockford's* swamp up to his neck. It's pretty certain who actually wrote it, and parts of it are probably actionable – not that Runcie intends to do anything but maintain a dignified silence; he knew about it two weeks before publication. The suspected author of the poisoned preface is an academic so cloistered he probably didn't realise what he was getting into, how he was being used. The traditional Crockford leg-pull developed a vicious twist.

From the Foreign Office: for years past the FO has been trying to get Downing Street to reverse its policy on charging overseas students through the nose. Like cuts in the BBC overseas services, the policy is costing us an immeasurable fortune in influence and goodwill. But Mrs T. and her golfers remain obstinately deaf. Economies have been made and that's that. Poor Geoffrey Howe has to suffer the indignity of Mrs T. finishing all his sentences for him – the way *she* wants to hear them.

It is also reported that Denis Thatcher was seated at table next to a lady whose husband was sightless. 'How long has your husband been blind?' asks Denis. 'Since birth, actually.' 'My word – then he's never *seen* Margaret.'

From a fellow veteran in the broadcasting trade: do I remember, some twelve years ago, when I was anchoring a radio programme called News Desk, and I was approached by some organisation which claimed to be doing a survey of 'opinion formers'? Indeed I remember being most flattered at the time. So a man with a briefcase full of forms came to my office and asked me a lot of questions about how I felt on the subject of multinational corporations. Did I think they were an exploitive capitalist conspiracy, etc.? In fact I had no particular opinions about them but said they had never done me any harm – on the contrary, as a foreign correspondent I had always found their representatives most hospitable and swift with the refreshing flagon. The interview plodded on into mounting apathy. There was a parting handshake and nothing more. I never even saw a paragraph in the *Financial Times* to say that 1% of opinion formers couldn't care less about multinational corporations.

'Well,' says my fellow veteran, 'I had one of those interviews, too, at about the same time. Mine was all about Vietnam, on which *you* were supposed to be the great expert at that time. *I* was meant to be specialising in multinationals. The guy got his files mixed up. The fact is, you and I were being positively vetted by the spooks. No wonder we both got through innocent.'

And I never knew they cared.

The evening's Jewish joke. The President of the United States is on a world tour. He calls on the Pope in the Vatican. On the Pope's desk the President sees a bright red telephone, set apart. 'Is that . . .?' 'Yes, Mr President, it is my personal hot-line to the All Highest.' 'Might I use it, very briefly, to make an enquiry?' 'Of course, Mr President, but I must warn you that on account of the advanced technology required we must make a charge of $500.'

The money changes hands – American Express will do nicely – and a call is made the contents of which I may not disclose for reasons of confidentiality.

A day later the President arrives in Israel and is received by the Chief Rabbi. Upon his desk, an identical bright red telephone. Can it be . . .? 'But of course, Mr President – my hot-line to Him who cannot be named. Please use it to make a call!' 'Would $500 cover the cost?' 'You are very generous, Mr President, but here *local* calls are only a dime.'

December 8th

During a weekend of uproar over the *Crockford's* affair
it is the high Tory *Sunday Telegraph* that lets an extremely
shabby cat out of the bag: that there *was* a conspiracy
reaching from the Tory party and its allies in the Synod
to the still-anonymous author of the preface with the object
of starting a landslide to unseat Runcie and preventing John
Habgood of York from taking his place. But on the Tuesday
morning I am rung up, in bed, by the *Evening Standard* with
the news that Canon Dr Gareth Bennett of New College,
Oxford – after persistently denying he wrote the preface –
has gassed himself in his car. Now the prank has really
curdled, but there's not much I can add from this distance.
Surely Pattinson will at last have to come out of hiding and
say something.

Later, he does. He and his opposite number from the
Church Commissioners admit to having invited Bennett
to do the preface, and to having printed it as received.
Well, golly, now we know who the assassin was, and who
hired him, only the assassin's assassinated himself. Runcie
expresses dignified regrets but still very properly declines
to join his enemies in the swamp. Talk about confidentiality! Bennett was not only a member of one of the inner
committees of the Synod, and of the Crown Appointments
Commission, but a personal adviser and speechwriter to the
Archbishop – and used his position to smear them all. Lying
to several of my colleagues in the religious reporting business
is a relatively minor peccadillo.

December 9–10th

A frenzy of 'phone calls, typing and thrusting copy into
the hands of leather-clad dispatch riders. One advantage

of being in the religious affairs trade is that there's so little competition. Paper A orders a thousand words and then cancels ('Sorry, old boy, scandal over the Test match in Pakistan . . .'); but never mind, a stylistic tweak or two and the words rush off to paper B. But I decline to do a late night monologue on TV. The producer books me for Radio 4's Sunday programme. Monday is Thought for the Day. I'm looking forward to our post–Christmas retreat in Carfury.

December 11th

Now that I have had my hair cut my hat fits much better.

December 13th

I appear as court jester on the Sunday show, which is mainly a chance to make remarks about the *Crockford's* case. Since one can only hope to get across one or two simple points on these occasions, I argue that it's a sorry distraction from the solid pastoral work being done all over the country by vicars and congregations regardless of ecclesiastical party. A BBC taxi fetches me and takes me home, but the relaxed adagio of the seventh day has been shattered beyond repair.

December 14th

Monday does nothing to restore my bio-rhythms, begin-ning as it does with a Thought for the Day. The truth is, I haven't really got one. So, since cricket is in the news, I spin out a little fantasia on the quarrel between Mike Gatting, the England captain, and the Pakistani umpire. I tell the listeners that my immediate sympathy is with the umpire who strove so valiantly to have the match, if not the entire series, called off. Anything that can be done to help stamp out this ludicrous pantomime masquerading as a sport must be applauded; especially when the effect of the alleged sport is not only the embitterment of Commonwealth relations but the suspension of normal traffic on the Third Programme for days on end. Either the thing is a game – which is nothing without an element of fun – or it isn't. The operative word is 'to play', and it is hard to see anything remotely playful about it any more. National pride and professional reward have turned it, like diplomacy, into a form of warfare conducted by other means. If Englishmen and Pakistanis feel they have to play cricket together, why don't they send eleven players each, mix them up, draw out teams regardless of nationality, and play for the sake of the game.

Desperate for some reference to religion in all this, I then imagine sermons being preached in our great public schools reminding the boys that 'when the Great Umpire gives you out it's no use disputing the verdict – there's nothing for it but to take up your bat and walk!' But as a piece of popular theology I fear it is a bit thin. My producer rings up afterwards to request more piety next time, please. But annoyingly, the broadcast annoys hardly anyone. Not a single angry letter, which is very disappointing.

In the evening, Sylvia and I pack up minor suitcases and catch an overcrowded train to Cambridge, where I am to sing for my supper. A dining club from Bedford has hired the hall at King's for its annual banquet. The King's Singers provide a floor show (too much barbershop, I thought; and they resolutely refuse a single encore) while I propose an elaborate toast 'To Christmas!' Thank goodness my local Reform rabbi has told me two new Jewish jokes. Food: so-so.

When it is over the Bedfordians climb into monstrous motor-coaches and are driven home. Sylvia and I have been booked into a Cambridge hotel, which is comfortable enough, though I am glad not to be paying for it.

English hotels nowadays simply are not worth the money. They become more reasonable at weekends, but during the week they are full of itinerant salesmen and lawyers signing away their expenses. The food comes out of plastic bags and the bedrooms are crowded with electric kettles and packets of tea, coffee, cocoa, soup, biscuits and peppermint creams so that you can enjoy a solitary dorm feast while watching provincial television. This particular hotel has been converted from a row of incommensurable houses knocked together, so that one fights one's way round it like a rat in a laboratory maze – up three steps, down four steps, through the fourth fire-door on the right and there you are in the laundry room instead of the bar. It helps to convince Sylvia that there really is no place like home and that life with the unquiet suitcase is not always as glamorous as she suspected.

In the morning Cambridge emerges damp, foggy and traffic-jammed. 'A pretty place, but remote,' I called it once before. As an Oxford man I miss the snugness and the bells.

December 16–17–18th

Successive evening parties at Dolphin Square, Hampstead Garden Suburb and the BBC: the first with a lady journalist from our Washington past, the second with our doctor (where we always sing carols round a tree alarmingly decorated with real burning candles), and the third with the radio religious broadcasting department, whose chief, David Winter, seems to have acquired Our Lord's knack of turning water into decent wine and converting a few loaves and fishes into a pretty adequate feast for multitudes. Compared with the inhibited tea parties the department used to give when I first joined it, things are swinging in religious show-biz these days, and I quite enjoyed it.

146

December 21st

My last Thought for the month (thank goodness), and my orders are to think pious for a change. So I take Christmas carols as my theme and hold up Good King Wenceslas as a proper example of Christian charity for this day and age. Then a stampede to Euston to catch a train up to Birmingham where (for some reason) Radio 4 has decided John Timpson and I shall celebrate Christmas morning for two solid hours, four days in advance. Then we can lie in bed and listen to ourselves when the great day dawns.

The BBC's fun palace at Pebble Mill is one of its less depressing premises. The studio has been decorated in keeping with the festive season, a passable buffet has been laid on, and a bowl of steaming punch designed by somebody to cheer without inebriating us. But alas, with punch as with computers, the lesson is 'rubbish in – rubbish out'. Timpson and I take one sip each and stick to the canteen coffee.

Goodness knows how we contrive to fill the time. We do have the choir of Coventry Cathedral who manage to sing without that deep-frozen tone characteristic of most Anglican trebles. When asked if they wouldn't rather be singing pop, they respond with a unanimous yes! Then the resident reverend lurches in with a sack of toys for the boys (I get a bottle of Hermitage and a book by Timpson – Timpson gets a bottle of Scotch and a book by me). 'Tom Forrest' of the Archers reads the nativity story in a folksy accent, which turns out to be his normal way of speaking. Two other actors perform John Julius Norwich's jolly skit on 'The Twelve Days of Christmas' – and Timpson and I exchange anecdotes. At intervals our producer plays recordings of church bells, obsessively, because she is being persecuted by the bell-ringers of Britain who regard Christmas morning as being their special preserve and are indignant at having Timpers and me taking it over. In honour of my Washington connection a recording is dug out of the carillon of the National Cathedral there – indeed, it stood at the bottom of my garden. Unfortunately the tune selected to greet this joyful morn is 'Auprès de ma blonde', which being translated, goes:

> In bed with a woman,
> Oh, it's great, it's great, it's great!
> In bed with a woman,
> Oh, it's great to sleep!

Glossing this over, I tell the story of an alleged friend who played the trombone in a military band and shot the regimental mascot in the backside with a pellet of frozen spittle. When we go off the air the Reverend Santa Claus says, 'I liked the trombone story but I don't believe a word of it.' 'Just how I feel about the nativity story,' I tell him.

Eventually we package up our fake Christmas morning and go our separate ways – Timpson back to deepest Norfolk, fondling his bottle of Scotch. But he will have to keep the top on till he gets home. He has to drive the last few miles from the station and there are breathalyser men lurking behind every hedge.

December 22nd

Having spent Monday afternoon in a studio with Timpson pretending it was Christmas morning, I have to spend Tuesday morning in another studio with Brian Redhead pretending it is New Year's Eve. The idea is to review the year in the churches, but Redhead is such an enthusiast for the subject himself that I don't get to say what I wanted to say. Never mind. The world will keep turning much the same as ever, little recking what Redhead and I have said or left unsaid.

December 24th

To Sylvia's triumph, Raymond and Diana arrive from Cornwall with the infant Jennet and an open epiphany is held in the sitting-room, with friends and neighbours casually invited in to admire her and drink her health. The tree goes up, presents are piled round it, there's an aroma from the kitchen of onions stuck with cloves infusing the bread sauce.

Soon after eleven at night we walk up to St Jude-on-the-Hill for midnight mass – and it very nearly *is* the mass, St Jude being deeply into smells and bells. Not very Quaker, I admit, but it's nice to have a good sing for a change.

December 25th

Like (I suspect) most people, I sleep through the Timpson/Priestand show. There were fifteen people in the house last night, then the mass, and this takes some recovering from. Our feast is usually late on Christmas Day, and we fill the time preparing the table (which means clearing Sylvia's studio to set it up in), gathering the clan (which, with auxiliaries, will be ten this year), and opening presents. I am long past expecting anything heart-stopping: it's not that I have everything, but the things I would still like – a French horn, a grand piano, a new car – are beyond the resources of anybody I know, so I am grateful for relatively small things which I could buy for myself but can't be bothered to track down. This year, a pocket magnifying glass for reading the small print in the A–Z, and some cassettes of Bach cantatas. There's about two hundred of them and I can never remember which I have or haven't got, but Sylvia checked through

them and came up with half a dozen new ones including the
No. 140 *Wachet auf* whose opening figures fill me with joy
. . . Diana presented me with four books of jokes about
sheep-farming, or rather four books of *the* joke about sheep-
farming which is they roll over and die at the least excuse or
none at all. Very hilarious.

The feast goes well, Sylvia having mastered the art of
mass catering to a high standard. As usual we end up playing handball with balloons across the table, the idea being to
avoid (or *not* avoid, according to taste) landing the balloon on
the burning candles. This year's crackers, from Habitat, were
disappointing. The snaps didn't snap, the hats didn't fit, the
trinkets were junk and the riddles were rotten. I think I shall
set up as a riddle-writer myself.

Q: Why should we describe Mrs Thatcher as the greatest
English woman since Elizabeth the First?
A: Because she might be listening.

Oliver and Natasha are off in Rome and Jennet's Ed
is visiting his parents up country: otherwise we have a
full house. Jennet – Jennet the First, that is – is putting on
weight after her ordeal, which is a good sign despite one or
two minor queries about the scanner readings. Andreas looks
the complete dashing young executive, with Sally as his –
and our – darling. Diana the last, first with the grandchild
and patently content with her country life and husband. God
be thanked for them all, their love for us and, most loyally,
for one another.

December 27th

The family disperses. Having tidied up we follow Raymond,
Diana and Jennet the Second down to Cornwall. An
uneventful drive, except the discovery that 'they' (who?)

have driven a mysterious tunnel under the harmless little town of Saltash, so that we are likely never to see it again. And, arrived at Penzance, huge pillars have been moulded in the ground near the railway station, indicating that the A30 road is about to leap into the air and come to earth again who knows where? It is hard to see the point of bypassing Penzance, since you can't go much further without falling off into the Atlantic. The only thing beyond Penzance is the parking lot at Land's End, a tourist attraction (for singularly ill-informed tourists) for about two months in the year. Still, if the farmers have to be stopped from growing too many crops I suppose the surest way of doing this is to put motorways over their fields.

Nothing much seems to have happened in Carfury. Ken, the policeman who works as the coroner's righthand man, is deep in a case of treasure trove involving three 3,000-year-old gold bracelets discovered on a nearby farm. There's some quarrel about who is entitled to the reward, complicated by the fact that very few lawyers specialise in this rare corner of the law. The front page of *The Cornishman* reports three cases in one week of people being swept off local beaches and drowned. What with the weather and the modern equivalent of the twelve days of Christmas, it is doubtful there'll be any fresh fish to be had at Newlyn during our stay.

December 28th–January 9th

Appalling Cornish weather. Nonstop gales and varying densities of rain. Cats refuse to go out for fear of being blown over the fields to Ding Dong. So we eat and sleep and read and cuddle ourselves by the stove, all the cosier for the elemental uproar outside.

My holiday task is to collect the material for a lecture I have been commissioned to give by the Haberdashers' Company – an annual event known as the Golden Lecture.

Knowing they would expect something moral or theological I determined to step out of character and tell them the Shocking Scandal of St Buryan for a change.

St Buryan (named after an Irish lady missionary called Beriana circa 550 AD) is the central parish of the Land's End peninsula, with a fine fifteenth-century church and a ninety-foot tower. Originally it was a humble Celtic chapel, but when Athelstan evicted the Danes in 936 he established it as a royal foundation with a dean and three prebends, from which it somehow assumed the status of a Royal Peculiar with the rights of Greater Sanctuary, subject only to the King and immune to episcopal jurisdiction – though the bishops of Exeter thought otherwise. As the centuries wore on the kings appointed royal favourites who enjoyed the income but never went near the place. Paganism and depravity were rampant throughout the deanery. Things rose to a leisurely climax between 1300 and 1350, with cases at law, bloodshed in the churchyard, an invasion by armed knights and – in 1336 – the excommunication of the entire deanery by Bishop Grandisson standing on top of St Michael's Mount and shouting the words of commination across the sea. For a time Buryan was subdued by the threat of Hellfire. Grandisson entered the church in triumph and preached on the text 'All ye like sheep have gone astray' in English, French, Latin and Cornish. But within a few years things were as bad as ever. 'These men are constituted almost like wild beasts,' confided the bishop to his brother of Worcester: 'They lustfully couple in every prohibited degree and are divorced in every lawful one.'

And so it went on for another *six hundred years*, with absentee courtiers pocketing the tithes and poor curates, at five quid a year, holding the occasional service. My favourite dean of Buryan was the last, Fitzroy Henry Stanhope – an old soldier who had lost a leg at Waterloo and was unordainable until the royal family got their creature the Bishop of Cork to priest him. Stanhope turned up in

Buryan once in forty-seven years, just long enough to read the Thirty-nine Articles. But from 1817 to 1864 he collected at least £1,000 a year from the living. Small wonder that he left it a hotbed of Methodists and (they do still say) practitioners of the black arts.

The present rector tells me that one curious feature of his congregation – which is large for this day and age – is the unusual majority of men attending. Now what would the women be up to? My friend the local antiquary has seen naked ladies dancing round the stone circle at Boscawen-Un. 'Local ladies?' 'I really couldn't say, Gerald. I didn't stop to ask.' Meanwhile the Buryan choir continues to wear scarlet in token of its royal foundation. I alarmed the rector by pointing out that under Athelstan's charter, *his* part of the bargain was to say a hundred masses and a hundred psalters for the king's soul.

With a little more information from the diocesan exorcist – if he will give it – this should make a lecture with a moral: people complain when the Church meddles in politics; but how much worse when politicians meddle in the Church.

December 10th

And so back to London and a stack of letters, bills and newspapers. The Church of England's unholy alliance of Anglo-Catholics and Evangelicals has been scattered by a row over homosexuals in the priesthood – something to which the Anglo-Catholics are inclined but the Evangelicals (on the whole) not. Sundry bishops have been declaring that it's their rule not to ordain *practising* gays; but I know quite well one vicar who has a live-in acolyte-cum-housekeeper. Both of them are spikier than the Pope, and the parish has put up with it for years. For one thing, the vicarage buffets are superb.

Graham Turner has a well-researched article in the *Sunday*

Telegraph on how the intellectual elite detests Mrs T. The only specimens he could find who didn't were Anthony Powell, Francis Bacon and Kingsley Amis, none of whom I would expect to find on the shelves or walls of Dunroamin, Dulwich. Though it might be rather fun if Bacon were to do the PM for the National Portrait Gallery. Most of the elitists (including the Warnocks) express my own feelings – a kind of allergy that starts in the head and rapidly affects the stomach.

Given time, which she seems quite likely to get in the present ludicrous state of the Opposition, I have little doubt that Mrs T.'s economics will considerably enrich the nation as a whole – though the achievement is less impressive if you make comparisons with continental Europe (lack of interest in foreigners is an essential part of Thatcherism) and I fear it will do little or nothing for the unemployed underclass in places like Belfast, Liverpool and Glasgow. You might have thought that British culture and scholarship would have excited the lady's patriotism, but she seems to have no concern for them, regarding the arts and universities as auxiliaries of the business world at best. The word 'fascist' is not to be used carelessly, but there's a kind of paranoia towards intellectual independence; as there is towards local government.

And I think the golfing class has badly miscalculated people's feelings about the National Health Service. I don't think people have ever felt that British Coal, British Gas, British Telecom or Airways were really *theirs*; but the Health Service is something different, something not to be messed about with, rather like the Church of England. You start life in it and you end life in it, and in between it comforts your aches and pains and shelters you at your weakest. We made it (we feel) and we resent anyone taking it apart. It is no use Mrs T. reeling off her alleged facts and figures showing how much more her government is supposed to have done than any previous government. Everyone has some first-hand story to tell about wards being closed and operations delayed. It is hard to find anyone within the service itself who will give evidence for the defence.

January 12th

The dilemma of my class of Englishman is that the more spontaneous you are, the more time you have to spend feeling guilty later. Take the case of this junior foreign minister, David Mellor, visiting the Gaza Strip, who sees the Israelis roughing up a Palestinian and says the equivalent of, 'Oh, I say there, that's not good enough!' A rare example of a British politician reacting like you and me and saying what he feels. But what an uproar follows! Arrogant! Interfering! Neo-colonialist and implicitly anti-semitic! Myself, I try to avoid making public comments on the Middle East for fear of being denounced and intimidated by one side or both. Years ago, on the air, I made some remark which was less than totally pro-Israel. Within hours a rota of protest phone-ins had been set in motion and I received a letter from a neighbour reminding me it might have been a bomb instead. So I stick to pontificating about Afghanistan and Cambodia.

The above paragraph squeezed in on my way to recording a quite different event which probably shows me up in an even more shameful light. I cannot help being convulsed by a small item in *The Times* beginning 'A 16-stone fishmonger who committed serious sexual acts with three soldiers after posing as a woman major was jailed for 18 months yesterday.' Lewd, juvenile and heterosexist it may be of me; but I find the picture mind-blowing. Imagine the soldiers' glee at scoring with a member of the officer-class – however bulky – only to find . . . Oh dear, I *am* ashamed at my imagination. The Army says it is not going to punish the depraved trio, thinking, no doubt, that the ridicule of the barracks is bad enough. As for the fishy majorette, the charges did not, apparently, include bringing discredit upon the Queen's uniform.

Today's more serious business includes being interviewed by a young American woman who is doing a thesis on religious journalism. Students like her come to my house at the rate of about four a year and I have to work hard persuading them it is not enough to believe that God has called you to be His prophet – indeed, any such conception has to be aborted instantly. The task is to be a good journalist in a field where there are all too few.

The offer arrives of another Hon DD, this time from Hull. I am tempted to write back saying I now await Hell and Halifax – but no, it is very kind of them and I accept. I am beginning to worry about all these robes and hoods. I have a splendid sky-blue cloak from the Open University and an apricot hood from Manchester Polytechnic; goodness knows what regalia will follow from St Andrews and Hull. But what is the etiquette for wearing which where? Ecclesiastical occasions might present an opportunity, but my fellow Quakers might disapprove of such 'carnal' ostentation. I remember once processing down an aisle alongside a bearded academic who seemed to be dressed as Santa Claus. 'Overdoing it a bit, old chap, aren't we?' I murmured. 'Alas, Toronto . . .' he replied.

January 15th

Rosenkavalier at the ENO with George and Irene Engle. Not a great performance, I'm afraid. Tired old scenery. Conductor in a hurry. Ochs too coarse and Mrs Field Marshal insufficiently autumnal. But such a great score, with the horn choir in splendid form, that it still leaves me tingling.

January 16th

A frustrated attempt at one of our artistic Saturday mornings. We try to see the Chinese terracotta warriors, but a frozen queue stretches halfway across Vincent Square so we divert to the Tate where the queue for Beatrix Potter is warm but still too long. After contemplating some junk sculpture we join a much shorter queue for lunch and then go home to make marmalade.

You never know how this annual ritual is going to work out. Sometimes you have to boil the stuff for two hours before it will set, taking saucer after saucer of samples into the garden for the tell-tale wrinkle test. This time we ignore it for thirty minutes and *bingo* – ready to bottle. We only eat it on Saturdays and Sundays, so it lasts all the year and we would sooner starve than resort to the insipid commercial variety.

January 17th

A gastronomic treat. Pink grapefruit and new marmalade for breakfast (in bed). Roast beef for lunch. To dinner with the Engles (to swap photographs of our separate Nile cruises) and are feasted on artichoke soup followed by pheasant. Apart from Egyptian memories George has a seventeenth-century translation of Livy to gloat over – a snip lately snapped up in a bookshop in Chipping Campden; Irene and Sylvia compare and contrast the marital status of assorted children, but the law of confidentiality seals my lips against further disclosure. What a myth it is that children are ever 'off one's hands'. In any case, mothers have sticky fingers.

January 19th

One of those days when even if nothing much really gets done, at least the different passages of wasted time fit neatly together giving the impression of masterful organisation and a full diary.

First, a chap from Melksham in Wiltshire wants to see me about talking to his local council of churches. Could I come on March 7th? As I want to go down to Cornwall then to put in two weeks' uninterrupted writing on 'the novel', I could in fact stop off on the way. But what to talk about? So we get together in the coffee shop of the National Gallery, which is a very convenient place for meeting people in. If you want to fill in time before or after your chat, you can stroll among the pictures which (it's so easy to forget) are very, very good indeed. There's a quartet of Veroneses which send me into a trance; an air of sumptuousness throughout.

Second, a publisher's lunch (that's what publishers are for, after publishing). A nice publisher's lady from Hutchinson feeds me on clam chowder and salmon and discusses plans for promoting the paperback of the autobiography in April. It will mean the usual bout of prancing round the local radio stations and bookshops and though I doubt whether it has any significant effect on sales, the busy-ness keeps the publisher happy and gets me the reputation of being a cooperative author.

Third, up to the shabby headquarters of BBC religious broadcasting to discuss with Ron Farrow the gathering of material for our two programmes on the Lambeth Conference of the Anglican Communion which is being held, perversely, in Canterbury in July. It will involve a week in Rome immediately after Easter, when the steering committee has a warmup and we can get at some of the episcopal stars, like Desmond Tutu, without having to compete with a dozen other interviewers. Could Sylvia come and bring her sketchbook? Yes, of course.

I return home by way of the birdseed shop in Goodge Street. In fact it is an old-fashioned ironmonger's selling buckets and nails and hurricane lamps, too. But the floor is cluttered with sacks of dog-biscuits and guinea-pig pellets and corn-chandler's sweepings which are ideal for the garden birds in winter. After earnest discussion the proprietor and I agree that there is no way of preventing the squirrels from getting half of it, however. I keep throwing Cadbury the Siamese out to grab our local marauder, but the squirrel has outwitted him so often that the cat has stopped trying. The birds aren't afraid of him either. Our garden disproves the claim that you can't have birds and cats. You can have birds and incompetent cats.

January 20th

Just before Christmas I wrote to the BBC begging them to change the music they use on 1500 metres to fill the five-minute gap between the end of World Service programmes and the opening of Radio 4 at 5.45 a.m. It is always the same: Elegy (I would call it) by a Brokenhearted Guitarist upon the Death of his Only Daughter Aged Six. I'm often awake at that hour with my spirits at a low ebb, and my eyes fill with tears as the guitar throbs its way through a succession of minor thirds, falling sixths, all the clichés in the book of tear-jerkers. It's followed, I admit, by a rousing medley of British folksongs ('Annie Laurie' played against 'Danny Boy' and 'Scotland the Brave' against 'Men of Harlech', most ingeniously) – but by that time I am ready to shoot myself and fumbling for the revolver. Couldn't they, for the sake of us dawn depressives, play something less enervating – say, Ravel's Daybreak?

Someone staggeringly senior in the BBC writes back to say that they'd have to *pay* Ravel (who I thought was dead) but the guitarist is free. Presumably he's one of those black-market musicians they pick up on street corners in Hamburg. The very senior person promises to dry my tears in the spring when the clocks go forward and the gap won't need filling. In the meantime, will I be terribly brave and he'll find something happier for next winter? 'Don't shoot! We need you!' he urges.

January 21st

I am the evening's floor show at a seminar of about thirty high fliers from British Petroleum held, agreeably, at the Compleat Angler by the river at Marlow. Most are British but there are several Americans and at least one Norwegian. It seems to be a kind of corporate battle-course with computers instead of machine-guns. In that context I suppose I am virtually the chaplain, so I give them the latest development of my thoughts on the moral responsibility of business. They take it pretty well, apart from two chemists who say they are fed up with being told they are poisoning the air and the water and why does nobody ever thank them for their wonderful discoveries? Like, I suggest, the upholstery foam that suffocates fire victims; and the aerosol gas that's destroying the ozone layer? Not us! they cry. But the trouble is, unless somebody takes his eye from the microscope and raises it to Heaven occasionally, science and technology simply *will* do what they *can* do and leave the rest of us to pay the cost. Scientists nowadays try to insist that all they do is measure and handle the data, as if they were purely objective. But if you look into the history and sociology of science you run into some rather embarrassing problems about what kind of an enterprise it really is – why at certain times it asks certain questions but not others. Sooner or later a theologian has to make some kind of assertion as to what he considers the truth; but scientists have rather given up the question of truth, and if they go too far along that road they are going to find themselves – in some cases already have found themselves – enslaved by those who want to politicise or commercialise science and harness it to the purposes of the state, the party or the company. *Some* superior value will assert itself over our choices, so it had better be a good one. Enter the Christian doctrine of man and creation.

What *I* get out of these occasions is the opportunity to meet the kind of people I don't usually meet. After I'd done my preaching we had an hour or two at the bar – somewhat more solemn than usual because of the American presence.

January 22nd

Wake up in the Angler to vile weather. Drive home to find the roof leaking and the roof man up his ladder saying depressing things about the price of sheet lead. I thought the bottom had dropped out of that market – or was it copper?

Cheered up by headline in our local paper RABBI SCHOOL'S ROWDINESS ENRAGES NEIGHBOURS. Only in Golder's Green do you get rowdy rabbis.

January 23rd

Too bloody awful a day to go anywhere or do anything. The central heating has failed, so I devote my efforts to lighting and tending the open fire to keep the house warm. But I have to go down the lane to the shops for two or three things like firelighters and am horrified to discover that they have seen me coming and put up the price of typewriter ribbons again. I buy about six a year and the price is *always* higher than last time. I have empty boxes proving that not so long ago they were £1.00, £1.20, £1.80. Today they are £2.20. What possible justification can there be for this? Have guerrillas occupied the ink-mines in Madagascar? One of these days I shall complain and the assistant will sneer, 'There's not the demand now, you see. Most people use word-processors.' But not me, never, never, never. Writing is the craft of making meaningful marks with ink on sheets of paper, not playing Space Invaders.

January 24th

To Friends for Meeting, where I find myself 'sitting up' with Kitty Slack as presiding Elders. Also with Kitty's dog which maintains an air of pious contemplation for all but the last five minutes, at which point he senses the departure of the Holy Spirit and begins to whine. I feel moved to speak a little ministry myself on the sympathy between animals and saints, mentioning St Kevin in whose praying hands a blackbird laid her egg – the saint remaining at prayer until the egg hatched.

Andreas rings to say he and Sally are moving to Harpenden, a place I have yet to envisage. Jennet and Ed come to lunch and say they are thinking of going to Chippenham. Well, it's better than Australia. Jennet has put on more weight and grown some punkish hair after the chemical devastation. Diana telephones from Cornwall to say that both her Jerseys, Amy and Marcia, have calved and she has been on a course in cheese, butter and yoghourt making. There is an excellent Cornish cheese called Yarg, made by a family called Gray who simply spelt their name backwards. But it won't work for Diana Priestland-Hearn. Perhaps she will make Cambornebert.

January 25th

Good: a contract for a new book arrives for signature, with an advance to follow. Bad: it is so soggy outside that I cannot set foot in the garden and the lawn looks like a fillet of wet fish laid out on a slab. But it is mild, the first snowdrop is out and the birds – always eager to be misled – are making springtime noises which they will have to retract if February lives up to its usual depressing reputation.

Fergie is preggers and the BBC loyally announces universal joy, interviewing American tourists outside Buckingham Palace (monarchists to a woman) and studiously rearranging the order of succession to the throne. It is just as well Prince Edward has got himself a Really Useful Job. Sylvia is scathing. She thinks there are already far too many minor royals. 'But Queen Victoria had nine children and thirty-seven great-grandchildren in her own lifetime,' I remind her. 'She was lucky not to have the BBC as well,' is the retort.

In the evening the Corporation (Really Useful as ever to an ungrateful Establishment) does its duty in the form of a long interview with Mrs Thatcher by David Dimbleby. She sails through it emerging without a scratch. The quickness of the statistics deceive the ear, but I don't think I believe any of them. In particular, I don't believe her assertion that if you help the successful to become even more successful their money will 'trickle down' to the unsuccessful. The secret of the rich is that they keep their money to themselves. And she seems to have the weird idea that it is the job of universities not only to conduct industrial research but develop it commercially.

Someone who fancies his contacts told me the other day that Mrs T. wants the evangelical Michael Baughen of Chester to be the next Canterbury.

January 26th

The roof man is back with sheets of expensive lead to repair the roof. I try to write a fairly intense sermon for Holy Week with him hammering away over my head. Even without him it would be a delicate matter, because the sermon has been commissioned for a church in Newlyn, Cornwall, whose vicar calls himself 'Father' (signifying Anglo-Catholic sympathies) and I'm on a bit of an anti-clerical wave at the moment. 'Call no man Father on earth,' says Matthew XXIII and the thing that stands out in the Easter story as far as I am concerned is that Mary Magdalene thought the risen Christ was the gardener – He was Everyman, He was a man you met walking along the road or cooking fish by the lake. And as for the Last Supper: it's all very well to make a special priestly event of the bread and wine, but what about getting down and washing people's feet – which is every bit as mandatory as far as I can see? However, I'm doing this for John Halkes, director of the Newlyn Art Gallery, who is a member of the congregation and reading for the priesthood himself. So I shall be gentle. Bang, bang, bang overhead.

January 28th

Rain, rain, rain overhead – thank goodness the roof is fixed. The cats, disdaining to wet their aristocratic fur, explode in wild pursuit up and down the stairs. According to the wireless, Cornwall is swamped, which must be a misery for Diana's calves.

I have my first interview to do for Ron Farrow's programmes about the Lambeth Conference. It's with the agreeable (and Most Reverend) Donald Arden who spent almost forty years in Africa, ending up as Archbishop of Central Africa – almost as good as being Patriarch of Antioch and all the East. By coincidence it turned out that he was once curate at Nettleden-with-Potten-End, my home village in Hertfordshire, and vividly remembered the antics of the Home Guard of which my late father was second-in-command.

Among other things, I asked how one coped with

running an ex-colonial church in a newly independent Marxist African state. 'Sense of humour,' said the archbishop, and told me the story of how a diocesan of his had dealt with a law closing all the churches and banning services anywhere. 'But he read the law carefully and discovered that it did permit praying for the sick. So every Sunday one member of each congregation took to his bed and all the others crowded into the bedroom to pray for him. Miraculously almost all the invalids were up and about the next day.'

Though its parties have improved, the accommodation of BBC religious broadcasting has gravely deteriorated since my day. We used to have highly desirable offices at the front of the flagship on Langham Place. But then the department was told it would have to move to temporary accommodation while the offices were repainted; and when it tried to move back, Religion found that a mob from Finance had squatted. Nobody dares push Finance around, so the reverend broadcasters are still moping amongst the rag trade in Clipstone Street, served (or rather neglected) by an early prototype of the first elevator, hand-operated by a shell-shocked veteran of Dunkirk. Someone in BBC management has obviously calculated that charity, patience and mortification are compulsory virtues for Christians.

After a pub lunch I cross over to the South Bank where there's a photo-call for alleged celebrities taking part in the Hoffnung Comedy Concert on Feb. 13th. Gerard Hoffnung's widow Annetta has asked me to tootle a beer bottle in the Surprise Symphony. We rally in a wine bar called The Archduke – assorted musicians, actors, odds and ends like me, Desmond Wilcox, Bamber Gascoigne, Donald Swan – and for more than an hour arrange ourselves in the ludicrous postures loved by cameramen. 'Now just look natural!' they cry. 'Gerald, put your elbow where your chin was and your leg in Donald's lap . . . Now just one more with your trousers falling down . . . *lovely!*'

Then the man from the *Independent* turns up late, fresh from the Old Bailey, and we do it all over again, getting surlier and surlier – all except Donald who is cooperatively manic throughout. Afterwards he and I have a cosy little chat about depression.

On the way home I buy a bargain pineapple at Waterloo Station, not so much to eat as for Sylvia to paint. Most of the fruit and vegetables in our house come to the table a bit withered, having first had to pose in the studio. Once, years ago, Sylvia reproached the children for leaving a bowl of peaches to rot. 'Oh,' they said, 'we thought they were Still Life.'

The mail has arrived, bringing a summons from the Royal Free Hospital to report on February 16th to have my varicose veins done. I have been over three years on the waiting list. Well, it should make a heart-warming item for this diary which has been somewhat neglectful of medical drama for the past few weeks.

January 29th

A crew turns up from Channel 4 News to interview me about Whither the Church of England. Ah, whither indeed? At least not down the drain, I assure them. News of its death-throes has been greatly exaggerated. As always, Sylvia dreads having a camera crew in the house; lack of privacy aside, the place is not big and a crew takes up a great deal of room. But this one arrives promptly, works quickly and gets away in little over half an hour – though I shall be lucky to see myself on the screen for as much as one minute (*later: an overestimate*). For a shy person, having a crew in one's home must be rather like having a longboat full of Vikings land on your private beach. Me, of course, I lie back and enjoy it.

Elegants and Millingtons and Robert Fox's wife Marianne are coming to dinner tomorrow, so I am packed off to the trout farm to buy smoked fish and watercress. It is a miserable, murky drive up the A41, though more restful than the motorway. I turn on the radio and sing along with a schools' music class. They are rehearsing the choruses for a musical – quite tricky but a lot more fun for the kids than the Merry Month of May stuff they did when I – ah! – was young.

The winner, so far, in this year's Small-Earthquake-Not-Many-Dead headline contest: HUNGARY SNUBS ROMANIA (*The Times*). Not many offended.

More seriously there is a huge rumpus about the six Birmingham pub bombers having their appeal rejected, with the English huffing as if no policeman could ever beat up a prisoner and the Irish puffing as if no Irishman could possibly plant a bomb: the English totally failing to appreciate the Irish national myth, and the Irish failing to appreciate the English dislike of being blown up. To call it reciprocal hypocrisy would imply that both sides were not utterly sincere. The trouble is they are – blinded with sincerity. We both lack the French gift of cynicism.

January 30th

The final recording of the commentary to the CTVC 'homeless' film. It's always quite fun hitting the shots with the right remarks – one eye on the script and the other on the monitor screen; but frankly I am bored with the project by now. Goodness knows where, if anywhere, it will get shown. At least radio and newspaper work blow away quickly in the wind, enabling you to hurry on to the next bit of nonsense. But television drags on and on and on.

The dinner party is delightful: smoked salmon, pheasant, gooseberry fool (can that be the right spelling? I look it up and Oxford says '*especially* gooseberry fool').

There are seven of us, a good number. No gossip I dare record.

January 31st

Friends' Meeting. Towards the end, one dear lady Friend gets up and gives tongue to a confession of self-reproach. So, after a pause, I rise to recall the good Abbé de Tourville and his repeated assurance: 'Remember, God loves you just as you are.' It infuriated him in his gentle way that so many people could not get this into their heads but would keep trying to imitate this or that saint, who they were patently not. This ministry seems exactly the right thing, for afterwards three Friends come to me and say it spoke to their conditions. It's nice when that happens and I'm sure it is more worthwhile than singing hymns and reciting the Service Book.

We take an elderly widowed Friend home with us for lunch (boiled salt beef and carrots). She's a mere eighty-five and wears jolly crimson tights. May I be as bright in twenty-four years time, but I doubt it.

February 1st

Chris Donovan, my GP, has been trying to bully me for months into losing weight. Having failed, he refers me to a cardiologist in Harley Street who says the blood pressure isn't dangerously high – yet – but did I realise the risks of a stroke? So much nastier than a heart attack. All right, all right, I'll be good. I'll stop *writing* so much about food. This manuscript is littered with pheasants.

February 3rd

To Oxford to interview George Appleton, once the Anglican Archbishop in Jerusalem. A lovable and holy old chap who is not afraid of a spot of heresy. When I asked if it were possible to convince Muslims that Christians really did worship one God and not three, he said, 'Well, I'm not at all sure of that myself.' After a distinctly universalist passage I asked, 'But surely you believe that Christianity is in some sense the *best* religion?' To which he replied 'Yes, for Christians.' Which is exactly right.

The Anglican Communion prides itself on having handed over its colonies to the natives. But as these interviews continue I realise that the generation of Appleton and Arden was achieving an understanding with other faiths that could only suffer a setback when indigenous bishops took over and felt they had to prove themselves more Anglican than the English.

Appleton, who was a Somerset gardener's son, began his ministry in Stepney, where nine out of ten parishioners were Jewish. 'I used to sit in the church with the door open, and they all came to have a chat with me about their problems.' Then he went out to Burma, entirely surrounded by Buddhists. He had to translate his prayer book into Burmese, 'And believe me, it really makes you think what it means – if anything – when you have to turn Tudor English into a language like that.' In Jerusalem there had been a double stimulus: Christians having to live under Jewish authority for a change, but most of those Christians regarding themselves first and foremost as Arabs. No wonder Bishop George has a broad mind. He is certainly my kind of churchman, but I fear it is a kind that will be shouted down in years to come, as the voice of the protestant evangelist is heard in the land.

Still very soggy out of doors, but now we have some early yellow crocuses showing.

February 5th

What an action-packed afternoon: I'm quite exhausted. At lunchtime I saunter into the back garden where my nose tells me instantly that Golder's Green Crematorium is holding an *auto-da-fé*. It's not an aroma of roasting flesh but of blazing coffins – not unlike a house on fire. From the front of the house, looking across the Jewish cemetery, it is all too clear to see: lazy black smoke rolling off the top of the tower and drifting in all directions. This doesn't happen often. On the whole the Crematorium is a dignified neighbour generating nothing worse than the occasional sombre traffic jam. Having checked with my neighbour that this is going too far, I type a strong letter to the director of the Crematorium advising him to have his gas ovens serviced.

As I return from posting the letter I find six people scrambling over the fence into the cemetery. About five years ago hooligans climbed in during the night and painted swastikas on the tombstones, so the fence was put up to keep them out. But then a branch fell off an oak tree (the one the owls hoot in) and crushed a gap which hasn't been fixed for months. I question the intruders, who have bunches of flowers and say they have come all the way from Turkey only to find the main gate locked. So I write another cross letter to the Jewish burial society telling them to look after their dead properly.

Back at my desk I look out of the window and see the damn squirrel is raiding the tits' nut-basket again. So I send the reluctant Cadbury after him. As usual, Cadbury mistimes his charge and finds himself face-to-face with the ginger-and-white tom who lords it over the neighbourhood. In a flash Cadbury does a U-turn, back through the cat flap, up the stairs and under the bed, leaving me to rush out and disperse the tom and the squirrel. An Honorary Doctor of Divinity (elect) shouldn't have to do jobs like this.

Tonight more opera: *Hansel and Gretel* by Engelbert Humperdinck I.

February 6th

Engelbert sent us home humming the tunes. A man of one opera he may have been, but a real smasheroo at that. No thanks, however, to David Pountney, the ENO director who chose to mount Dvořák's *Rusalka* as a Freudian fantasy. This time not only does he put the woodcutter's family onto a 1950s council estate, but the fourteen angels have to materialise during the entr'acte as the milkman, the postman, the policeman and other assorted neighbours, coated in whitewash. The sandman and the dew fairy become meths-drinking tramps. I hope I live long enough to witness the Romantic Counter-Reformation that must surely come, with a proper gingerbread house and a wood with trees instead of a bleak municipal playground.

February 7th

Dragged into Broadcasting House as dawn is breaking, to be interviewed by Margaret Howard about Marghanita Laski who has just died. Everyone calls her an atheist, but she certainly wasn't an aggressive one. She was an unbeliever who couldn't leave faith alone. I remember her lecturing the religious broadcasting department about its duties; praising us for attending to people's need for the irrational (she thought this was quite legitimate and would, she said, settle for an Anglican funeral herself); but castigating us for being reluctant to stand in judgment against society. Cruelty, sexual permissiveness – why weren't we doing something about *that*? It showed up the essential Jewishness that Marghanita pretended to have renounced, though I think it would be an insult to her integrity to claim that she was really a believer but didn't know it. I think God *needs* some disbelief or faith couldn't be voluntary and we could not love Him.

Marghanita was the arch Hampstead Intellectual – the sort who gives elitism a good name – with a mind like a set of surgical instruments elegantly wielded. The last time I interviewed her she asked, over the telephone, whether I would stay for tea: 'and crumpets, I am told, are appropriate for the time of year'. I thought this was a joke, but said that would be splendid. And when I got to her house at the summit of Hampstead Heath, there they were in the kitchen: Earl Gray tea and crumpets crisp on the outside and oozing butter from every pore. 'I do not consume them myself,' she said in her meticulous voice, 'but I made enquiries as to their preparation and am assured they are as they should be.' One could not have done better at Buckingham Palace. There was even a touch of majesty about it, for Marghanita had class.

Louis Heren, Monica Furlong and Russell Burlingham (a professional tracker-down of rare books) come to Sunday lunch. Russell has even managed to track down an obscure volume on *Cheese-making for the Aspiring Dairymaid* demanded by Diana down in Cornwall. But I promised to cut down on writing about food.

February 8th

An envelope arrives addressed to Sylvia. Inside, a card saying the Prime Minister and Mr Denis Thatcher request the pleasure of the company of Mr and Mrs Priestland at a reception at No. 10 Downing Street on February 29th. Which is curious. I wonder why? What can it be about? What a good thing this diary won't have been published or I should certainly never have been asked.

February 9th

Hurricane warnings, and by breakfast it is blowing 105 miles an hour at Land's End. But no 'phone calls from Carfury, so I assume the roof is still on. Up here in London it doesn't seem as bad as last October. The fury rises and falls in invisible waves instead of blasting us continuously for hour after hour.

Two more radio interviews to be done: one with George Simms, at the other end of a line in Dublin, and the other face-to-face with Dehqani-Tafti, the exiled Anglican Bishop of Iran. Simms I had met in Armagh when he was Primate of All Ireland. Tafti recalled meeting me long ago in Isfahan in the days of wine and roses.

The Simms interview is marred by a strange whining noise which gradually intrudes into the conversation. When I persuade the Archbishop to ask whether it can be eliminated, an Irish voice can be heard in the distance remarking, 'Sure, it's only the water pipes that do it all the time.' So I pass another message to find the nearest tap and try turning it on and off a few times; and they do; and it stops; at which the Irish declare themselves vastly impressed with the BBC's long-range mastery of their plumbing. Simms and I then resume talking about St Columba and the seniority of the Celtic Church over the upstart introduced from Rome by Augustine.

Tafti, who I feared was going to be dull, turns out to be inspired. He's been shot at, slandered, harassed, had a son murdered by Muslim fanatics and his wife wounded, but Christians seem at their best when persecuted. I ask him if he doesn't find the Church of England too smug? 'They have their persecution, too,' he says, 'the persecution of being ignored.' As he sees it, the C. of E. has been ahead of the times on most of the big social and moral issues of the past fifty years. He is not impressed by the yapping of wee John·Gummer that the church has failed to stand up against 'our condom culture'. Come to think of it, it wasn't the Church that put French letter ads on TV – it was Mr Gummer's government.

Looking back, I haven't had a lot to say about God in this diary. We don't seem to have been in touch very often over the past year – but that's often the way it is. He gives you intensive treatment for a few months and then drifts off, presumably to look after some more urgent cases, but leaving you with enough to keep going on till next time – though sometimes, as a tease, barely enough.

February 10th

A rather dud interview – I won't say who with. Probably my fault, but you can probe around for ages trying to hit some spot that will produce a jerk of reaction, and never find one. But I have provoked a retired Oxford professor who writes to reprove me for saying – in my interview with Channel 4 News the other day – that I thought Richard Harries would make a splendid Archbishop of Canterbury. The professor thinks this is stooping almost as low as Peterborough in the *Daily Telegraph* – mere gossip and an embarrassment to the good bishop. So I write back saying it can't have been the first time Harries has been told that. Or, if it is, he'll soon be used to hearing it.

February 11th

Yet another bishop to interview – this time a Scottish one, Alistair Haggart from Edinburgh and, like most of the Scots divines who have come my way, thoroughly enlightened and lucid. 'The Anglican Church is not a church for fanatics and fundamentalists. It has to develop its understanding of scripture in the light of its experience of the world. And the nature of its authority is curiously feminine. It cannot be exercised in the dominant masculine way of Rome, but through patience and conciliation and persuasion.' A warm, humorous man. It is a great pleasure listening to him.

Hurd the Home Secretary had a go at the General Synod last night. So did Gummer who disgracefully accused the Archbishop of York of countenancing the promotion of homosexuality – but who is to take Gummer seriously any more?

Hurd was progressive enough to say he did not share the view that the Church had no right to comment on social and political matters, but churchmen who did so had 'come down from the pulpit' and must be ready to take the rough and tumble of political debate. (Fair enough, and they have never expected anything else.) Then Hurd went on to complain, as if it were some new discovery, that people who committed violent crime appeared to have no human feelings for their victims: 'It is as if for them neither the Old nor the New Testament had been written . . . What society most desperately needs from the churches today is a clear, definite and repeated statement of personal morality.' Then there was more about the Church helping to supply 'social cohesion' by insisting on 'individual standards'. In failing to do this the Church was abdicating a duty which it alone could perform and which no one else could make to the health and happiness of our society.

It is something of a relief to find the government laying off the broadcasters for a change – they used to be the agents of immorality – but maybe Hurd reckons he has plans already in the pipeline to fix them. Make a free-for-all of the air waves, shatter the BBC and the IBA system, and politicians will have nothing more to fear from the ensuing triviality. But I can't see it doing much for 'social cohesion' towards which I should have thought the BBC made the biggest single contribution.

Hurd's speech sounds to me like a mixture of seduction and excuse-making. After nearly ten years of Thatcherism the country is richer (or some of it is) but no more virtuous. It must be the fault of those dreadful liberal bishops who have abandoned their role as the Tory party at prayer.

Actually, it is not all Thatcher's fault, either. Morals started drifting in their present direction long before she came on the scene and certainly before the present bench of bishops. But if preaching is held to be so effective – and Hurd seems to be asking for more and louder sermons on the Ten Commandments – it is not the church which now commands the national pulpit but the state. Whom do we see and hear, day after day, but Mrs T. and her repertory company? The Church has been a declining influence in the land since, at the latest, the First World War. Hurd is fooling himself if he thinks the bishops could be or have been a significant moral influence in his lifetime or mine. But perhaps he is only scapegoating.

Why the Church has become so ineffective is another question. It has something to do with the steady takeover of former church functions like education, social welfare and the policing of behaviour by the state. In many ways that is admirable. But the state has never paid much attention to the moral aspects of the duties it has assumed, to moral and religious instruction in the schools, and it is now becoming increasingly impatient with the welfare function. It has made it harder and harder for the family to survive and for mothers to give full-time care to young children if they wish to do so. It is hollow for the state to demand that the church exalt values which are ignored by the state's own instruments.

In so far as the church itself is partly to blame, I blame it for having been too slow to adopt a modern theology that makes sense, too slow to take an interest in social and political affairs. The clergy seemed almost incapable of responding intelligently to the hammer blows of Marx, Freud, of science and two World Wars. The Age of Reason took a long time to work its way down to the people, but by the time they had learnt to read, there was little left on the shelves but rationalism. For most people (especially men) church has become boring and irrelevant. Mothers often do their best when the children are little, but the kids won't keep going to church if Dad never comes with them. There are much more interesting things to do on Sundays.

It exasperates me that the Thatcherites keep pointing at *individual* sin and demanding *personal* morality. It's not that these don't matter, but what about the power behind the sins of society? What about wicked policies? If you want social cohesion, you cannot ignore them. What hope is there for the moral individual when his life and family are bashed and battered by a greedy and indifferent economy, a political regime which worships the Trinity of Growth, Profitability and the GNP?

In the end, however, the kind of morality Hurd is talking about does not rely upon religion. It is natural morality, the product of an orderly, just and rational way of life. Any pagan can be morally good and I know plenty of unbelievers and non-churchgoers who are better than I. Christianity is not a moral lecture – it is not about being good. It is about the knowing and showing of the love of God, and moral behaviour (which is a great deal more than not hitting old ladies) is one of the fruits of love. We do not gather it from the pulpit. We gather it from our experience of Incarnation and Crucifixion and Resurrection and the Life Everlasting. And when we experience it, there follow Repentance, Forgiveness and Grace which is nothing else than the Love of God, received, understood and returned. I am not convinced that church is really the best place to find all this; but if Mr Hurd wants to hear it preached about, he can hear it in 40,000 churches, chapels and meeting-houses any week he cares. It can do the Church nothing but good to be mentioned in ministers' speeches like this. But I wonder what the church attendance record of the cabinet is like?

February 12th

Up in the morning early because, by appointment, the gasman cometh to mend the central heating. But no he doesn't. Instead, the gasman's supervisor rings up to say they are having a Day of Action. Splendid! Action is what we need. Sorry, 'action' means they aren't working at all but might come next Thursday.

Apologetic letter from the Crematorium saying they have spent £122,000 on new equipment and realise that it still doesn't work properly. Rest assured etc. . . . In the meantime, smoke gets in our eyes.

February 13th

The day of the Hoffnung concert. I am involved in this because Sylvia was at Hornsey College of Art with Gerard Hoffnung – in a way, I stole her off him, but made amends by serving as Gerard's best man when he married Annetta. And then, having started these crazy concerts, he went and died while we were away in India. Anyway, I have to rehearse my bottle-blowing at the Festival Hall in the morning and perform in the evening. There's seven of us blowers, including Desmond Wilcox, John Lill, Patrick Moore and me – plus the Philharmonia Orchestra who, like all orchestral musicians, are the salt of the earth, the best company in the world. Did you know that the entire trombone section of the Philharmonia (*and* the tuba) are *professors* of their instrument? No wonder they sound so authoritative when they hoist those golden bazookas onto their shoulders and prophesy to the four corners of the known world.

There's a limited number of musical jokes and the Hoffnung repertoire exploits all of them as far as they'll go. It can't be done too often and it's a bit of a gamble whether the public has had enough; but apparently not, because the two evenings are practically sold out. Two items I had not seen before: the Concerto d'Amore in which two violin soloists begin by hating each other and end up falling in love, and the Disconcerto which is a battle between exhibitionist pianist and equally exhibitionist conductor. I will be modest about our Surprise Symphony, except to say that my bottle 'spoke' every time – unlike some I will not mention.

Anyway, it's always a pleasure to be in the Festival Hall, which to my mind is the one successful member of the South Bank complex – unlike that melancholy mausoleum the Hayward Gallery, to which Sylvia and I betook ourselves between rehearsal and concert to see Lucian Freud. You can't deny it any more, he's a great painter, beginning as a draughtsman and working his way up, becoming more and more painterly (Sylvia's word – a sheer master of paintstuff, I suppose). And underlying it all, a flawless anatomist: he knows what all the muscles you can't see are doing.

A painting is what it is – an arrangement of masses and colours. Freud's organisation of these takes you back into the Renaissance. But once you've got human beings in the composition you can't avoid, not necessarily a story, but a past. Who is this man, this woman? What have they been through to look like that? Their bodies are too particular, too used, too human to be regarded as mere models. They all seem to be recovering from something. The later ones from love, the earlier ones from some bad dream they can hardly speak of.

But as if it weren't enough to be superb at this hardest form of painting, which Freud always calls 'naked' not 'nude', he keeps interjecting, 'Do you think I couldn't paint a horse if I wanted to? Then look at this. Or a kitchen sink? Or a potted plant? Or a row of houses? Or all of them together?'

Some people, I guess, will see Freud's naked women as rude and exploitive: hire a woman at so much an hour, strip her of modesty and exhibit every detail from pudenda to floppy breasts. But that's not how it strikes me. This is how we are – yes, *we*, for you can't overlook his equal frankness about what lies between male legs, too. It would be exploitive to use the people as the basis for soft studio eroticism; but every one of these paintings shows a respect for the subject as she or he really is, and in a way the slavish camera can never catch.

February 15th

A golden spring day in the middle of February, but I still don't trust my natal month. In any case, tomorrow it's off to the Royal Free to have my varicose veins done. I pay off outstanding bills, buy a Tom Sharpe paperback and Evelyn Waugh's *Helena* and bring this diary up to date. Checking through my records I find I have been on the waiting list for the operation for three years nine months.

February 16–18th

I have been warned about candidates for operations being bounced in and out of their beds like standby passengers at airports, but the Royal Free keeps its word and in I go as scheduled, clutching the junior suitcase I use for weekends. 'That *all* you got?' says the man in the bed opposite. His name is Charlie, a jobbing builder from Enfield, who is constantly shocked by the parsimoniousness of the middle classes. 'D'you know,' he says, having decided I represent the acceptable face of the bourgeoisie, 'they'll do up the outside of a house, new windows, new doors, carriage lamps and all that; but inside there's nothing! Just a coffee table and two or three chairs – some of them made of metal and straw. Now, where's your comfy three-piece suite? Where's your table for tea, your china cabinet, your piano, your knick-knacks? Me, I've got several genuine oil paintings, painted by hand by French art students, of the Eiffel Tower and the Arch de Triumph. But my middle-class neighbours just have one scribbly picture that's mostly paper, and it's been *printed*. By someone called 'ackney.'

'Hockney?'

'Thassit. 'ockney. Anyway, nothing to it. Typical middle class, all mean and stingy.'

I confess that *my* house is a bit like that, and make the excuse that, being big, I need lots of empty space to move about in. Charlie says that as a bachelor he likes lots of furniture to keep him company. He'd been in the navy towards the end of the war, mostly round the coasts of Africa. That wasn't one of my territories but we get on well enough, swapping descriptions of places the other has never been to. After a while Charlie says, 'You know, Gerald, for a famous person you're all right.'

'What's the difference', I ask, 'when we're both laid out under the knife?'

The practical difference is that Charlie is back for operation number five on his prostate. It keeps growing back and he's become quite an expert on the surgical procedure: 'They go in up the penis, d'you see, and then you have this tube and this plastic bag and they wash you out till the blood stops.'

There are four beds in our section of the King Edward Ward. They are occupied by Charlie, me, Simon (a whisk-ery man who has had something humiliating done to his anus, lies on his stomach and doesn't care to talk about it) and a succession of corpselike old men who are also in for prostates. Charlie tries to encourage them.

'You'll still get an erection,' he promises, 'but you won't be able to ejaculate. That's what your prostate's for – ejacu-lation.' The corpselike old men give a croak of indifference. Charlie goes on, 'You soon get used to the nurses feeling you – I know most of them now from past visits – but it's not that easy to control yourself when one of these beautiful girl doctors leans over you and says, "D'you mind if I feel your penis?" Calls for self-discipline, that does.' Croak.

On the Tuesday I undergo the usual routine of being X-rayed, electrocardiographed, blood-tested and asked the same biographical questions by three successive juniors. Then my surgeon turns up with a troupe of students and draws veins with a felt-tipped marker all over the inside of my right leg which, it appears, is 'incompetent' and must be re-wired, though its brother on the left is spared. From time to time the surgeon pokes a question at one of the students, who remain dimly dumb. God help us if our lives are to be in *these* hands in a few years' time. Seeing there's nothing else to do when they've gone I put on my coat and trousers and shuffle to the lift, down to the ground floor and across the road to the Roebuck pub for a pint of ale. Being in hospital instils a pleasant sense of irresponsibility, I find. Later, Sylvia turns up with a splendidly irresponsible armful of lychees, grapes and peppermint creams which I guzzle till midnight while failing to laugh at Tom Sharpe. Across the ward Charlie – who never reads – is staring at the ceiling and singing softly to himself in the style of Flanagan or Allen.

Wednesday morning: we are all issued with our execution kits – a pair of paper knickers, a back-to-front nightgown that exposes our buttocks, and a notice reading NIL BY MOUTH, meaning Do Not Feed This Animal. After a while, Sister implants a tranquilising dart in every bottom and half-an-hour after that the tumbrils begin to roll.

Mine delivers me to a sort of frontier checkpoint where a uniformed immigration officer makes sure that I am who I claim to be (can there be people who try to gate-crash the operating table? probably there are), then I am brought to a halt in a starting-gate crowded with ladies whose one ambition is to put me to sleep. Which they do with total efficiency. I had been looking forward to filling the next fifty lines of this diary with vivid impressions of my out-of-the-body experience – of the tunnel of light, the paradise garden, the radiant figure in flowing robes, and the reluctant comeback to London NW3 ('They need you, Gerald . . . Sorry, some other time . . .'). But what in fact happens is that somebody sticks a needle in the back of my right hand, says it will start to feel cold; which it does; and CHONK – blackout!

The next thing I know is that Sylvia (aged about twenty-one, it seems to me) is kissing me awake and it is two hours later. There are mummy-wrappings round my leg, a slight ache in my groin, and someone has stolen my paper knickers. Otherwise, disappointingly, where *is* death's sting? When I need a pee I can even put my feet on the floor, stand up and toddle off to the loo. Andreas and Sally come to view the body in the evening and are almost as disappointed as I to find that their carefully banked-up sympathy has no object worthy of its warmth. Meanwhile Charlie, toting a milkman's basket containing a plastic bag of blood-red urine, is pottering about the ward briefing the latest intake of prostates.

Thursday: up, up and away within twenty-four hours of the operation. It might have been later had not Sylvia 'phoned the Ward Sister to explain that while she (Sylvia) was available to fetch me in the morning, she would have to stay at home after twelve because the gas man (celebrating a Day of Inaction presumably) was due to fix the boiler. 'I'm only doing this', says the nurse who bandages me up for the journey,' 'because of your gas man. Your wife seems to think he's rather special.'

Actually he is very ordinary, but at least he does come and there is almost more rejoicing over this than about my homecoming. For the next few days I stagger round the neighbourhood stealing firewood out of builders' skips and forcing the circulation through my mutilated leg. Pain is regarded as therapeutic these days.

February 23rd

What is one to do about a letter from a farm in Somerset which begins 'I hope you may be able to give me your advice about an allegorical matter'?

Well, one reads on, of course, to discover that the writer is a great admirer of the ballet *Swan Lake*. (What *am* I getting into?) The only trouble with it is that it is a mythical romantic tragedy instead of belonging to the 'superior' form of allegory – see Hosea, chapter XII, verse 10. (Oh dear, we have an attack of religion here, as well. 'I that am the Lord thy God have multiplied visions and used similitudes by the ministry of the prophets . . .')

My Somerset correspondent then cites the ballet writer Cyril Beaumont as arguing that a few adjustments to Act IV of *Swan Lake* would turn the story into a proper allegory 'depicting the nature, in depth, of the conflict between Good and Evil'. If only my good self will write a covering letter supporting this thesis my correspondent is sure that the present director of the Sadler's Wells ballet will be persuaded to fall into line. 'Surely a Hosea XII:10 allegory is a superior story-line to a myth? My commonsense tells me yes. So does II Corinthians IV:17–18.' (Trembling fingers disclose 'The things which are seen are temporal; but the things which are not seen are eternal'.) Don't feel any urgency about replying, says Mr X – he has already shelved the matter for thirty-eight years and another year or two wont hurt.

With desperate urgency I write to say that as far as I am concerned, the less music 'means' the better; and though I am all in favour of the Church sticking its nose into politics I believe passionately that it must keep its toes out of Tchaikowsky. Goodbye to another admirer, I'm afraid. Anyway, while professing lifelong devotion to my broadcasts, he calls me 'Priestley' throughout.

In the evening, my first social outing after the operation. Ken Howard – whom we met at his studio in Mousehole –

has invited me to sing for my supper at the Royal Academy Dining Club, which is throwing a banquet to mark the end of the Age of Chivalry exhibition.

I gather RA banquets have the reputation of becoming somewhat rowdy, but this one is pretty decorous. Indeed, it is hard to imagine Roger de Grey, Julian Trevelyan, Leonard Rosoman and Carel Weight (to name but a handful) being anything else. The closest to indecorous conduct is offered by Tom Phillips who staunchly refuses to wear a dinner jacket. Among my fellow guests are the Dean of Canterbury, one of whose stained-glass windows is the gem of the show, and the appetising Jill Neville, who long ago rented an attic in our house in Belsize Park and always introduces me as her former landlord.

Spectacular banquet hall. Goodish food. Excellent wines. Then I do my speech, flattering them for managing to make a living at all in this philistine country, I spin out my joke (of which Sylvia is pretty tired by now) about the messiness of artists – how artists' junk expands to fill not only the room available but a lot of other rooms where it has no business to be, rooms where a writer (the tidiest of creatures) may be trying to keep his notes and manuscripts in order and do a little quiet typing, etc., etc. Then, as a mediaeval touch, I try out a potted version of the Scandalous History of the Deanery of St Buryan, which they seem to enjoy. A glass or two of port and a stroll round the exhibition, unencumbered by public.

The leg, anaesthetised with port, does its job without a murmur; but Ken, who has driven up all the way from Cornwall, very kindly drives me home – where we catch Sylvia in her curlers and gossip till bedtime.

To be frank, Ken's painting is a bit old-fashioned for my taste – English Impressionist is a tag I think he'll accept – but, golly, he works hard and he knows how to do what he does and does it well *and sells it* – which, as I told the banqueteers, commands my deepest respect regardless of style. It isn't every painter who gets a 'phone call from America ordering 'your next twenty pictures, at gallery prices, as the focus of my collection'. And the story of Ken's marriage to Chrissie is so romantic you'd burst into tears if I told it – but I won't. He likes working in Cornwall because – although he realises the dangers of getting pixillated by the place – they do understand artists. The Cornish are cautious of 'furriners' generally, but as one of them told Ken, 'There's Cornish and there's furriners – but there's *artists*.' Never any difficulty in getting hold of a model, Ken says, down there.

February 26th

So now I am sixty-one and the wheel has come full circle, though I think I shall let it turn till the end of the month and our apotheosis at Downing Street. Ominously Sylvia has given me Nirad Chaudhuri's *Thy Hand, Great Anarch!* as a birthday present. Let us hope that Universal Darkness is *not* about to bury all.

I must take the book to Oxford and get Nirad to autograph it – as he did more than thirty years ago with my copy of his *Autobiography of an Unknown Indian*. That was when I was a green young correspondent in Delhi (my first solo assignment) and Nirad used to come almost daily to my office in the Cecil Hotel and warn me against becoming sentimental over Hinduism. This included sonorous recitations from the Sanskrit, which was rather like hearing an Orthodox archimandrite intoning the Liturgy of St John Chrysostom. Now he has produced another one thousand pages of impeccable English prose – and yet they have taken him only up to 1952. It would be a pity if he were not able to complete the century, on paper as well as in the flesh.

I shall never forget my parents' description of his visit to their cottage in the Chilterns, when at last (back in the fifties) the BBC and the British Council arranged his first visit to England. Nirad had always known everything about England: you could ask him where the Trocadero Restaurant was and he could give you precise instructions how to get there, but his friends were worried that the reality would not live up to his expectations. However he returned to Delhi after a few weeks to report that it had all been *precisely* as he'd known it would be, even down to my mother's China tea and cucumber sandwiches. What I did not learn until I got back to England myself was that Nirad had taken his tea perched on the mahogany cake-stand, which he had assumed to be some kind of antique stool, and from which my parents had thought it impolite to try and dislodge him. 'He sat there like a little bird,' said my mother, 'and twittered away for an hour about the history of the neighbourhood, which he seemed to know far better than we did. And then he shot off twirling his walking-stick and telling his guide from the British Council to hurry up. I don't think we got in a word ourselves.' I said I could imagine how it had been.

I spend a quiet birthday. Cards from the children, mostly vulgar ones with inscriptions inside apologising for the vulgarity and explaining you can't find anything else these days. Pheasant for supper. Meanwhile, outside, Nature is back-pedalling on the premature spring and sending down icy blasts from the north to retard it.

Looking back I confess I can't see a neatly architectured shape to the past twelve months; nevertheless I don't go along with Nirad's Popery about light dying before the uncreating word of Chaos. I might if I could only see it through my own eyes, but I see it through my wife's and children's, too. I see the light in Sylvia's painting, in Jennet's recovery, in Andreas's promotion, in Oliver's success as an impresario, in the birth of little Jennet and the delight of Diana. I can't say I have achieved much personally but it has all been extremely interesting – there's no such thing as experience wasted;

and although 'interesting' must sound rather a drab word with which to describe the gift of eternal life, I mean it as a compliment to my Creator. He (She?) seems incapable of setting up a situation which, if you explore it, doesn't lead somewhere unexpected – very often to a flash of love or beauty that makes you want more.

So more, please – if it be Thy will; and if not, I really have nothing to complain of. What a wild album of snapshots it has been! What a bundle of opportunities! What mercies, what pardons, what absurdities!

February 27th

This year's birthday treat is a tough one – like last year's, come to think of it. The ENO has scored a hit with its new production of *Billy Budd* – a work which still has some flaws in it after Britten's revision into two acts instead of four, but I must say it gripped me, and Sylvia, from first to last. It's the deep, relentless structuring of the music that does it, as if the sea were there heaving away beneath the stage throughout.

The big flaw is the character of Captain Vere, I think. For one thing, Forster and his fellow librettist couldn't quite bring themselves to say openly that Vere and Claggart are homosexually in love with Billy – the one paternally, the other sadistically. Then the two-act version deprives us of the opportunity to see Vere as the god-king inspiring his crew. It's hard to understand why Billy is so devoted to him. And it's just plain silly – when everyone else is in period costume – to have Vere dressed up as E.M. Forster in a dirty raincoat during the prologue and epilogue. After all, he very distinctly identifies himself as captain of the *Indomitable*, not as a Cambridge don. And *I* would have liked more ropes and spars to the scenery. And at the end, Billy should soar upwards to Heaven – not go down into Hell as this production seems to have him do.

Never mind, the chorus and orchestra were superb, and most of the minor parts. Thomas Allan as Billy sang magnificently but didn't look quite as appealing as the young Canadian I remember in the original cast. Richard van Allen as Claggart had the perfect black Iago-like voice but should have moved less regally. Vere – Philip Langridge – well, interesting, but not regal enough. It must be hard to act regal in a dirty raincoat. Come to think of it, Vere reproaches himself too much in his soliloquy. Billy *did* strike and kill a superior officer and in that day and age I don't see how anyone could have got him off hanging. One last niggle: the interview between Vere and Billy, which takes place offstage – or rather, in the orchestra – seems to me to lack the poignancy that's called for. It's God the Father sending his Son to the Cross, but I suppose for Britten it's so painful that he has to understate it. A mistake. Nevertheless I think back to that orchestra and those choruses and count myself fortunate to have been there. The house was sold out, not even standing room left.

February 28th

A quiet meeting at Friends, warmed by the news that two of the younger members are to get married in July. It will be the first wedding that our ageing congregation has had in five years.

Sylvia dutifully goes off to Bristol to see the first cabaret that Oliver has put on in the Theatre Royal. She returns after midnight to report a full house there, too, which is a great triumph. O. seems to have a flair for this kind of thing: identifying the market, judging the local taste, taking the risks, and conducting a highly successful one-man publicity operation. I don't think any of our children has done what we had planned for them; but what a joy when they pursue plans of their own and make them succeed, and are happy.

February 29th

The last day of this diary. I shall miss it. It's given my restless fingers something to say at moments when I've begun to doubt whether I'm still here. But 'I type – therefore I am'.

The wind is sharpening its knives in the tree outside my window. The weather forecasters, still smarting at their failure to announce last October's hurricane, have been trying to make our blood curdle with unlikely prophecies of blizzards for days past. One day they are bound to come true and the boffins will crow, 'We told you so!' Could it be tonight? A pity it is our soirée chez Thatcher. I would rather stay at home and keep warm.

We get to Whitehall a quarter of an hour early and waste the spare time pretending to be interested in the electric kettle department of an all-night drug store. Then through the barrier at the end of Downing Street, waving our invitation cards, and through that familiar doorway – which is immediately followed by a metal-detector gate which bleeps excitedly at every cigarette case and bunch of keys. Coats are then hung up on the sort of racks you see rag-trade people trundling up and down Mortimer Street.

Number Ten is far more palatial than you'd guess from the outside. It rambles on into all sorts of extensions and annexes through which the discreet may be admitted when they don't want to get their pictures in the papers. Past a bust of Disraeli, a portrait of Churchill at his most Churchillian by Frank Salisbury, and a haunting Brian Organ of the ruined Macmillan; up the stairs past a complete collection of photographed prime ministers. Detectives pretending to be butlers smile and beckon into the reception rooms.

'Mr and Mrs Gerald Priestland . . .'

Sylvia goes first and gets a gracious murmur. I get, 'But we haven't heard you so much on the air lately: haven't you retired or something?' Well, yes, I say and trot out the little joke about thirty-three years at the BBC feeling like a lifetime at an English public school which produces a hoot from Denis. 'But what are you doing now?' asks Mrs T. – looking exactly like Mrs T., in a stained-glass-window-blue tapestry dress. I write, I say, making typing gestures in the air. 'Ah yes, I know,' says the Prime Minister with a confidential gesture which implies that we'll say more about that later but will we please move on now.

The next room is full of people failing to recognise one another and wondering a) why on earth they've been asked and b) what theme, if any, is supposed to bind this human salad together. Certain groups are identifiable: clergy obviously, including Tony Higton who led the attack on homosexuals in the Synod, a sombre Catholic bishop, a black pastor, and an amazing prelate in a magenta soutane who must have taken time off from something by Verdi at the Coliseum. Then there are politicians: Douglas Hurd looking frayed at the edges and some rather dim back-bench Tories. Policemen exchanging masonic handshakes. Some ex-soldiers in regimental ties. Some select media people including Mrs T.'s favourite 'soft' interviewers like Jimmy Young and Michael Aspel. It's evident that this is a deliberately mixed bag chosen from various generic lists – Church, Education, The Party, Blacks, etc. – a dozen or so of each. I am not quite sure whether I am on the media list or the church list. Even less sure how I've got on either.

A variety of drinks is passed round. I get a disappointing-ly weak whisky and water, but the small eats are excellent, especially the chunks of prawn wrapped in pea-pods and the hot venison sausages.

Round the corner again is a pleasant little dining-room for a dozen, and beyond that an ornate banquet hall which would take three times as many. On the wall at one end, George II shows off his new fur coat ('Got it at Harrods – discount for royalty!' he seems to be saying); and over the fireplace a portrait of Nelson's second-in-command at Copenhagen. We chat to a retired general who raises money for soldiers' charities, and a grand dowager who has been in India to teach Indian ladies to arrange flowers – something which I can't imagine Indian ladies taking over from their servants.

At least it is quiet in the banquet room; but after a while we feel obliged to return to the festive throng, now about two hundred strong and rapidly clotting into its constituent groups – clergy talking to clergy and policemen to policemen. One of the black pastors serves me with a tract and tells us about the good works he and his wife are doing setting up Brownie packs in Brixton. Sylvia and I chat to the Aspels about good old days in Alexandra Palace, and to William Rees-Mogg who is full of praise for the *Independent* newspaper. William reckons it is on its way to becoming, eventually, number two to the *Telegraph* in the quality class.

The Prime Minister and Denis are mingling affably but we don't (daren't) push ourselves forward, though I had rehearsed mentally a few succinct outbursts about ceasing to wreck the broadcasting standards of the nation and not using the country as an experimental animal for vivisection.

What in fact happens is that it's eight o' clock and time to go. At which point a prime ministerial eye catches mine: 'Going off now, Mr Priestland? Tell me, are you writing something new for me to read?'

Well, yes, I say – thinking fearfully of certain passages I have put in these very pages – yes, and I shall be writing the end of it tomorrow. Should be out by the end of the year.

'That's splendid. I shall look forward to it so much.' Then, almost as if an invisible civil servant had slipped her the briefing notes, 'And may I recommend to you the chief Rabbi's latest book? And Cardinal Hume's? And then Richard Harries of Oxford sent me a book on C.S. Lewis.

And one called *Jacob's Ladder*. That's been my reading in your area this past year.'

Impressed with this attention to detail (had she read up, too, on flower arranging?) I hardly dared counter with one of my own. Gerard Hughes, Willie Vanstone, Philip Toynbee, I might have said. But mumbled ingratiatingly that I did have *most* of her favourites, and thank you for having us.

And this is the way the year ends: not with a bang but a simper.